Other Books by Susan Smith Nash

Poetry

Pornography (1992)

Grammar of the Margin Road (1992)

My Love is Apocalypse and Rhinestone (1993)

Liquid Babylon (1994)

A Veil in the Sand (1994)

Mind-Noir and El Siglo de Oro (1995)

A Paleontologist's Notebook (1995)

Fiction

Channel-Surfing the Apocalypse (1996)

Plays

Catfishes & Jackels (1997)

Doomsday Belly

by

Susan Smith Nash

"Doomsday Belly" originally appeared in the anthology *2000andWhat?* (Trip Street Press, 1996). Shorter versions of "Wildcatter" and "My Hairshirt Has Fleas" originally appeared in *Avec Sampler* (Avec Press, 1997). "Tia Erqueminia" originally appeared in the online journal *Perforations* (1998).

Front cover photograph by Howard Gelman

Back cover still from video by Catherine Kerley and Andrew Plummer

Cover and book design by Clare Rhinelander

Printed by McNaughton & Gunn on acid-free paper

Printed in the United States of America

ISBN 0-9639192-4-5

First Edition. 1998

Trip Street Press Books are distributed by:
Small Press Distribution
1341 Seventh Street
Berkeley, CA 94710-1403
1-800-869-7553 or 510-524-1668
spd@igc.apc.org

Trip Street Press • P.O. Box 190201 • San Francisco, CA 94119 USA

Doomsday Belly

Contents

The Trip Back

Stop One: Dead End After Church North of Red Rock Canyon

The ex-husband and I are within earshot of the whine of cars and trucks from I-40. We're on a road trip—a "Road Trip to Utopia." At least that was what he announced once he was completely confident he could manipulate me with guilt and get me to go on this weekend penance trip where he can lecture me about how "wrong" I have been and how he is "proud" of his behavior in the face of my "craziness" and rejection.

It's hot here in the July sun.

We're thinking about getting remarried.

We stop at the end of a road in the middle of sorghum, cotton, and wheat fields.

After the ex and I bail out of the truck, I stand on a bridge and look into the stagnant waters of a creek.

"It's really nice here, once you get used to the heat," he says.

"Once you pull off the sand burrs," I say. Now I've got them wrapped around my sandals and ankles. They sting. I'm trying my best to pull off the strands, but I can see it's not going to be easy.

Wilted leaves are rustling in the breeze. The locust trees, elms, sumac,

1

wild rye grass, and vines need a good rain.

A barbed wire fence stretches out over the creek. I wonder if a cow ever got tangled up in it during flood. Would the sheer dead weight of the thing tear down the fence?

"It looks like there's an old suitcase down there. Should I get it?" asks the ex. He stumbles down the eroded red sandstone bank.

A woman's bag is stuck on a bank near the bridge. It's half-open, as if it had been flung by some woman fed up with her own Road Trip to Utopia.

Right now, the stream is not in flood. The interstate highway is flooded with traffic, and it's about to go over the banks with speeding summer vacationers. I'm trying to convince myself that if I can be enough of a peacemaker, there won't be any more flood waters in my life.

It's too confusing. We're standing here, looking down at long, muddy banks, clusters of cattails, and wildflowers blooming in the sticky heat.

"Hey, why don't you just leave that woman's suitcase alone?" I ask. It is an attempt at assertiveness, but my voice doesn't carry. Who cares? I told him last night I wanted to remarry him. I'm looking down at my purse wondering how it will look half-buried in mud.

Stop Two: Geary, Oklahoma

She took my order and I wondered what kind of life she had experienced to give her those eyes, that hair, that refusing, suspicious attitude. She was an Oklahoman of indeterminate age, but not of indeterminate origin.

"Y'all want to get your drinks?" she asked. I ordered a Rocky Road sundae. It came in a Styrofoam coffee cup. Viva la difference. Viva la improvisation. This is a locally-owned Dairy Boy—not a Braum's or an I-40 mass-market chain stop along the highway river of dreams and Traveler's Aid. The people who live here tied up their boats and decided to stay out of the river. Or, maybe they were washed up here after an enormous flood. The Oil Boom was the flash flood that put many people here, the Bust was the drought that's still going on.

Rocky Road is exotica in a town that offers independence in the form of a deep-fat fryer and a stainless steel-coated freezer with a constantly changing inventory of ice cream and frozen treats, depending on what was on sale at the wholesaler's.

I always conjure up grandiose economic development schemes for places like this—places just far enough away from the interstate and the airports to miss the traffic in hope and Taiwan-minted loose change, but just close enough to the satellite dish to inspire the woman working here to appliqué Bart Simpson on a quilt for her grandson's birthday.

The woman is talking to another friend of equally indeterminate age, but sadly predetermined health. Lots of lard, bacon, homecooking— they would swear to their dying gasp that it's good for them, but I see it as the source of her liver spots, yellow-gray face, limp permed hair, torpid breasts, and bulging eyes.

"You need that thing 'bout as bad as I do," she's saying. It occurs to me that her Oklahoma twang and her local, relatively cryptic dialect are actually kind of cute. They're probably endangered. They would definitely be endangered if I had my way with my economic development schemes.

They're discussing something else.

"Did you hear about that woman they found out near Hydro? Decapitated—and no hands, no feet."

"I saw a guy last week pulling out of the bank parking lot in a Suburban that had aluminum foil all over the windows. God only knows what he was hiding in there."

Who am I kidding? I'd never in a million years be able to interest anyone here in my economic development ideas. A hog slaughterhouse like the one going up in Guymon is something they'd go for.

The cook brings our food to us. I notice a tattoo on his arm.

"Nice tattoo. Is that a hand?" I ask.

"No, it's a glove." He's lying. I want to run over to the booth where the woman and her friend are smoking cigarettes and drinking coffee so I can pull up their sleeves and see if they too have tattoos. What will they be? A decapitated head? A detached foot?

Yes, the perfect marks for members of the Geary Dairy Boy Devil Cult.

Well, that would explain the woman's bad complexion, strange bovine shape. Drinking blood at midnight is rough on your skin—even worse than down-home cooking. Mix that with late-night cattle mutilations and bestiality and you have what you see here.

Economic development—that's what we all need. Now, just tell me how I can get away.

Stop 3: The Water Trough

We're somewhere north of Seiling and southeast of Woodward. Five bald-faced head of cattle are staring me in the eye. They know the pain of castration, the thrill of anal de-worming. I'm not sure I really want to get to know these doomed bovines.

What would make an ear-tagged bovine stand hoof-deep in muck around a highly efficient windmill? It's as good a place as any to really chew the cud. A spotted one is switching his tail, now lowering his head. All I can think of are the news clips on CNN of the American backpacker who was gored to death last week at the annual bull run in Pamplona. Thank god these guys have been neutered. Thank god (thank the farmer) for the electric fence.

I downloaded two separate images from America OnLine. They were supplied by Reuters News Service, spin-doctored to satisfy the online customers, I suppose. In the 256-color, bit-mapped image, a college-age backpacker from the Midwest looked clean-cut beneath his hip little goatee and I felt incredibly sorry for him.

What happened?

He was from a small farming community and he must have known cows. He had to have known. But, in his urge to goatee and backpack away his identity, I guess he shaved off his common sense along with his unruly stubble.

I tend to blame the Europeans for his unnecessary death. If he hadn't been so eager to disown his American identity, shuck off his American roots, maybe he wouldn't have been so ridiculous as to run with picadored bulls on the way to their ritual slaughter. He should have read more Hemingway. Then he could have stuck with machine-gunning sharks and longing for androgynous females who dress like bullfighters. Then at least when he got gored he could call it love.

The cattle have backed off from the fence and are now facing me. I wonder if they think I'm one of those androgynous bullfighter-types who's wanting, more than anything, to make a statement about what it means to make a big showy display of valor in the face of insuperable odds. Or, if they sense in me my fascination with taking something right up to the edge and then seeing how the substance reacts. Heat it up in the crucible, see if it melts, explodes, evaporates or just lies there inert.

My breasts are too large to be androgynous anything. The female in me does not mean I can't be a bullfighter. The female bullfighters in Spain and Mexico have shown it's definitely not gender that determines the iconic symbol of danger and inevitable death.

The way I stand here on the side of the road, seeing the placid, pastoral yet quite temporary paradise existence of these creatures makes me realize their last dance will not allow them to show the heavens their rage at being selected to die to make someone else strong—a bullfighter, a people, a nationalist pride, or, in these cattle's case—to be ingested in the food chain.

I'm no bullfighter. If I am, it's simply at the slaughterhouse of dreams.

It's a good thing these guys are neutered. At least we have something in common.

Stop 4: Beaver, Oklahoma

I'm standing outside a nondescript concrete block building—it's some sort of ruined toolshed or machine shop. Who knows what machines they had to work on in Beaver, Oklahoma. Farming and drilling. Drilling in Beaver. Yes, that's a phrase that holds out the promise of a drive-thru adult video shop and a motel with mirrors on the ceiling, condom machine outside next to the Coke machine.

Rather than being a hotbed of prowling animal lust, Beaver reminds me of the small Oklahoma town my grandmother lived in. That's not to say she was a nuisance beast (like the beaver) or the neighborhood Peggy Lee voice of *Lady & The Tramp*. It's just to say that a name doesn't say much at all, especially not here, as we stand, listening to chirping sparrows and doves cooing and I'm reading THUG LIFE '95 spray-painted on the side of the dumpster next to the ruined toolshed.

Thug Life '95. What kind of thugs live here? Thug Beaver girls demanding service from their reticent, shy boyfriends? Thug Beaver women, fresh from the beauty salon all permed & tinted, ready to slap a little tail?

The ex proposed to me in Beaver. I faxed him instructions on how to do the marriage license, test, etc. That fax made him the butt of all the Beaver Motel staff jokes.

Slap a little tail, baby. Canoe on my pond.

He called me from every pay phone between Beaver and Oklahoma City to tell me he was on his way—we were getting married, baby. If I wasn't there, he left a message on my machine—it was an exciting time, that was for sure. I was ready to play thug beaver.

We're standing here now and we're to decide whether or not to spend the night at the same Beaver motel where I faxed him those How-To-Marry-Me instructions. The office has a little interlocking heart with plastic flowers nailed on the outside wall. I wonder if they put that up in hopes of turning it into a honeymoon hotel as well as a collapse-pit for exhausted drillers. If they do, I suggest more than a Hobby Lobby heart on the wall. They need the Poconos treatment—with heart-shaped bathtubs, camellia-scented bath gel, aromatic massage oil, champagne & fruit basket, terry bathrobes and towels with interlocking hearts on the edge.

No one faxed me HOW-TO-GET-A-DIVORCE instructions. No one needs lessons in running away. Or, maybe they do. Look at me.

Beavers were endangered once.

When my ex-husband and I married in the McClain County courthouse in Purcell, the signs announced we were in Horse Country. Obviously marrying in the land of horses somehow hexed us—three months later and we were both reeling from the old hoof-in-the-head wake-up call that something was seriously wrong with the marriage.

Horses are stupid animals. My dad had two on the acreage he had east of town. Charge and Verdi were once racehorses, but now they simply took their nervous temperaments out on anyone who didn't shove a bale of hay in their direction. My dad just let them run wild and free on 160 acres of prairie land. I guess they were watch horses, since they would menace anyone who came around and they threatened to give them a good swift kick in the head. My sister tried to ride Charge. He immediately threw her. She bled from her kidneys for a week.

Which do you do? Do you run away, or do you get back on and wait for the horse to throw you again? I'm not going to ask the ex what he thinks.

Maybe we'll remarry here.

Stop 5: Liberal, Kansas

The Korean owner of the Gateway Hotel we checked into at 10 P.M. after doing the strip on Saturday night in the biggest town in a 100–mile radius opened the door, presumably to check on the room to see if we had checked out. By now it was morning and I had just showered after a night of dreaming of rain leading into my house, water fading into my head. The experience was curiously resonant with this one.

"Sorry. Sorry." He had opened the door a crack, gotten a glimpse of my shoulders, towel-wrapped head.

"That was the Korean guy." I unstraddled the ex.

"I think it was a woman," he said.

This room is Spartan. Not even plastic cups next to the ice bucket. The bar featured a two-member country-western band singing *All My Ex's Live in Texas*. My ex is lying underneath me.

Last night we drank champagne and talked about when we could have our divorce set aside.

This morning, I'm thinking, "What was I, crazy?"

I'm wondering if we should deadbolt the door in case the Korean guy comes back around to see if we're finally left so he can rent the room to someone else sick of driving in this July southwest Kansas Never-Neverland of mirages and wavering unknowable relationships. I've started reading William James' *The Will to Believe* and I'm wondering, if I believe in a mirage, will that make it come real? If I believe in the image, however transient—the image of our restored, better-than-ever relationship—will that make it hold? keep still? hang with us? But, then how does that image overcome the reptilian-brain part of my head that screams, RUN, RUN, RUN!

"Get on your stomach. It's time for your back rub," says the ex.

In this room, everything of value is nailed down. The TV—the remote control—the cheap print of a pioneer's house on the wall. The towels are not as threadbare as the owners would like. I suspect they're stolen too often to get a chance to wear out. The furniture is durable, unbelievably square-edged—vintage early-'80s when the high prices of oil and gas precipitated migrations of laid-off steel-workers from Ohio, Pennsylvania, Michigan, where they worked in the oil business and lived in their cars until cheap overnight construction wonders like this Gateway Hotel could be thrown together. I remember what it looked like then—night sky flared alive with sparkling drilling rigs and new production. A well about every 640 acres. It was exciting.

Now Liberal, Kansas has a boarded-up Petroleum Club and a string of motels made of prefabricated sections glued or riveted together. I'm surprised the owners haven't offered this property to the state for rent as a minimum security prison.

I think of the people who have slept here, in this same room, during the '80s, who had opened the door to a boom, an opportunity, a new life, built from the old decaying beams and crumbling brick factories of the Rust Belt. Where are they now? Was their rebirth a good thing?

At least it gave them strength for a decade or so and some good times to think back on.

Everyone loves a boom. Everyone walks through the Gateway sooner or later.

Liberal's one dead-ass town.

Stop 6: Oklahoma State Highway 64, Somewhat East of Gate

It's surprisingly windy and cool out here—noon Sunday in July. I suggest we look at the clouds and imagine animal shapes. We've just been talking about our nightmare relatives and their deerhunter macho guns and ammo fetishes. I look up at the clouds and I see deer everywhere—one jumping over a fence, one looking at his mother, one drinking from the blue that could be water or sky or a glimpse of the eternal. A deer crossing sign is just ahead of us in the highway.

The deer they're referring to are of the more earthbound persuasion—they're not the type that fly through the heavens to be rearranged and metamorphosed when the water droplets and wind configure them into a storm or a blistering cloudless day. I suspect that in a few hours, the sky deer will have moved on just like we will, with our dilatory deer conversation, where all references to deer and to memories are also references to the divine, at least as we perceive it.

Since our talk has been about family and loss and feelings of being reunited, I'd like to contemplate the realm of perfection, the place where Dante's Beatrice is transfigured from a young, beautiful victim of plague or a pre-antibiotic-era infection into a symbol of wholeness and unity.

But, if I get off on the platonic or neo-platonic tangent, I lose sight of the here and now, the brown dirt and broken asphalt beneath my feet, the state highway linking east and west, daybreaks and dusks, beginnings and endings.

I imagine the place where real deer have eaten the tops off the farmer's newly-sprouted peas and green beans, and where another flesh-and-blood deer was plowed into by a tipsy guy in his new pick-up, gun rack along the back, who was just coming back from Liberal, Kansas and a fruitless attempt to get pussy and a new lease on life. He was probably busy looking at the sky deer and Beatrice peeking through the clouds when he plowed right into the side of that 10-point buck. It was the last thing both were to remember for a long, long time.

The ex offers me a chew from his new container of Skoal. "Won't it make me throw up?" I ask. I don't want to lose the Chester Cheetah Spicy Cheeze Fries I've wolfed down after a brief stop in Forgan, Oklahoma, near the Primera Iglesia Bautista and the local ammonium nitrate and diesel oil-plying feed and seed store. This is wheat country. It's also oil country. All the feed, seed, gas and oil money is locked up, though, in the names of people with northern European origins. A sign gives directions to their spreads:

> Geraland Long—S 3/4 miles
> Lloyd Heglin—S 1/2
> David Flowers—1/2 S
> Gary Graves—1 1/2 E
> A R. Kerns—1/2 W 1/4 N
> Terry Maphet—3 N 1/2 E
> Victor Maphet—2 N 1/2 W
> David Maphet—3 N 1/2 W

Where do the workers live? Probably in the woods with the deer who get nailed periodically by pickups and saltwater haul trucks. I wonder what life is like in the middle of the Maphet clan.

My ex-husband is trying to scare me by popping a pull-apart firecracker. He ruins the surprise by making a very obvious shadow.

He finally gets one to work. It sounds like a gun—one of far too small caliber to even make a deer flinch. I think back to the night before. A pickup with a gun rack turns off the highway and goes down the Maphet road. A cloud passing over casts a shadow in the shape of a deer. I turn to the ex and think about what would happen if I gave him a kiss. He reads my thoughts and startles me with another firecracker.

The deer-shaped cloud slowly drifts apart.

Stop 7: Alabaster Cawns State Park, Natural Bridge

We have just walked to the Scenic Overlook Point and looked down at the Natural Bridge. There is a sign which contains a brief geological history of the area. The caverns and the landforms were formed by groundwater dissolving the soluble gypsum layers, it says. What we are seeing is a good example of karst topography, named after a region in Yugoslavia.

The Natural Bridge has collapsed. Now it's a natural "Warning: Bridge Out" sight—a scene not too unusual in this State of bad roads and bad facilities. I hate that about Oklahoma. I need to go to the ladies' room, which is conveniently located near the vending machines and CAVE TOUR TICKET SALES office. I hope the flush works. The flush in the last State Park bathroom I visited was broken. What a drag.

The ex says he doesn't want to go on the hiking trail.

Not today, he says. Not in this sweltering heat.

This garden of eroded delights is best appreciated in the fall or winter. He's right. Who wants to hike half an hour to visit a collapsed bridge or an "Elephant Rock" sans trunk, or "The Giraffe" with a broken neck? Underground is no better. I think it's crazy that they lead tours through caves where the ceilings have the tendency to collapse, the walls crumble at the slightest pressure of a couple, tired of fighting, who decides to lean up against something for a bit of support or cooling off.

Montaigne wrote essays in his chateau, in rooms filled with assumptions that always collapsed on his head, but that was because he wanted them to collapse. What danger is there when a 16th-century aristocrat decides to rattle the pillars of his own castle? A lithe transitory existential doubt, not much more. Montaigne was no Samson, and reading his essays doesn't push you to any sort of apocalyptic edge, it simply liberates you from some of the confining assumptions you've been holding yourself back with for years and years. Shakespeare used Montaigne's essay, "On Cannibalism," for inspiration for

The Tempest, even modeling Caliban on the examples of humanity that Montaigne burst out of their cages. "O brave new world, that hath such people in it." Imagine the rage and primitive energy of a man-beast walking out of the ruins of a collapsed gypsum bridge or a French chateau or the Globe Theater at Stratford-on-Avon.

I'd hate to see us, driving around northwest Oklahoma, rattling our own beautiful construct to the point we're buried back at that cemetery we passed near Freedom. I'd hate to see our headstones—you, SAMSON, me, CALIBAN—just part of the karst topography, collapsing with the natural bridge.

The ex laughs at the sound of a woman with a thick Texas twang saying, "We don't have any previous spelunking experience."

She rattles off the list of required spelunking equipment: first aid kit, long sleeve shirt, gloves, water, rope, flashlight, canvas pants, boots, dry socks, lots of "D" batteries.

I would add a few things to her list: snakebite kit, helmet, aspirator, copy of Bunyan's *Pilgrim's Progress,* a copy of Thoreau's *Walden,* and a blank book with lots of pens in case she gets wedged in and has to write her own version of *Walden* or Emerson's *Self-Reliance* while the batteries fade, the ink runs out, and the cold sinks into her bones, reminding her of Donne's metaphysical sonnets, but reminding everyone else of Emerson's *Circles,* an attempt to make a truly tragic experience—starving to death in a cold, lonely cave—an excuse for aesthetics, or an inspiration for someone in a bad mood to say, "Why don't you just leave me the fuck ALONE!"

As the pen runs out of ink, there's nothing left to do but wait and hope—hope against hope—that the bridge will finally collapse right on top of her head.

Bridges don't really exist in nature anyway.

Stop 8: Hell-Sweet-Hell

The dog was outraged when I filled up a huge bowl with dog food, changed the water in his trough, and split. Not a walk or a combing or anything of the sort for two full days. I'm sure when I go back in the morning, I'll find he gnawed out his frustrations on his favorite chew toy, the garden hose.

On the way back, somewhere south of Okarche, the ex noticed a wide fan-pattern in the sky. He proceeded into a lengthy explanation that bored the shit out of me, mainly because I thought his purpose was to establish once and for all his supremacy in all things technical. He fucked up his computer and had to reformat the entire hard drive after one of those "I'm right, you're wrong" lectures. While he goes on and on, my head feels itself start to reformat. "Punish me. I deserve it." Grind, grind, grind goes the C-drive, reformatting.

We married. We divorced. The ex says, "I'll take you back if you change." I accepted some weird psychological take-or-pay contract with him when we married. Divorce did nothing to nullify it. Little did I know the fine print was inked on my ass.

Oklahoma's a good place to see the sights, isn't it?

Noches Paraguayas—Paraguayan Nights

Since the fall of the world's longest-running dictatorship, tourists no longer had to fear interrogation for taking a photograph of certain government buildings.

That's what all the guidebooks said, but I wasn't so sure, and I certainly wasn't taking any chances. The ghost of General Stroessner was creeping around in my dreams and I had to find it. I was fed up with life in the same old same old suburbanish upwardly mobile south-central U.S. town. I had announced to a number of friends that I was thinking about moving to South America. First, though, I had to check it out.

I wanted something spectacular. I wanted a place no one I knew had been. I wanted variety, difference, and a wake-up call for my hackneyed consciousness. And, if the truth were to be laid out utterly stripped bare, I wanted torture. And I didn't care if I didn't make it back to the U.S.

Okay. Maybe I didn't want real torture, just a sense of danger. I didn't want anything to do with stuff like peeled-back fingernails or electrodes to the genitals.

All the books said that torture was one of the specialties of the Conosur—the southern extreme of South America. In fact, Asunción even had a "Plaza de los Desaparecidos"—Plaza for the Disappeared Ones—next to the Parana River where supposedly they dumped the bodies which "reaparecieron" (reappeared) in Argentina.

Welcome to Paraguay.

My first impression was somewhat mundane. The airport was a modern edifice, about as big as the Oklahoma City airport in the mid-'70s. There was an aura of general placidity and laissez-faire. Words cannot express how disappointed I was that there were no M16-festooned guards in the airport in Asunción. In 1976 in Santa Cruz, Bolivia, there had been at least three.

In the Sao Paulo airport, three men in brown business suits had smiled at me like contented alligators. Brazilians, I thought. Shake hands and make speeches all day. I took American Airlines from Sao Paulo to Asunción, Paraguay. They say it's usually not a bad flight except when it's impossible to land due to the fog. Of course it happened to us. Circled circled circling and then we ended up in Rio, but not to hang out on beaches but to sit on the runway and refuel.

I saw the coast of Rio. Lovely place. Truly. The splendor of it echoed in my consciousness as we made the final approach to Asunción. Of course Paraguay was nothing like Rio or Sao Paulo. This was flat and in the interior part of the continent—a "Mediterranean" country, as they called it.

Thanks to the highly romanticized accounts of Paraguay that I had read over the last year, I expected everyone to be involved in some petty racket—if not cars, maybe tires or fake Rolex watches or fake designer clothing or something more interesting. All the literature said DON'T ASK where the stolen cars came from—which part of Brazil or Argentina and what insurance scam the owner decided to cash in on.

Long, low flat plain. Much green in the fields. Asunción's Silvio Pettirossi Airport looked disappointingly modern from the air—I had been hoping for a collection of palm-frond-roofed outbuildings and a palmetto-lined control tower and terminal building. How disappointing. In the Cayman Islands, the airport was partly open-air. We waited in line for customs in the thick, subtropical air. The line was moving very slowly. A woman was standing with her 6- or 8-year-old son. He was very quiet. Suddenly, he leaned over my carry-on bag, which I had placed on the floor next to my feet. He began to drool on it, heave, and then issue out big hunks of vomit on my brand-new Hartmann.

This occurred on the first day of my honeymoon to my first husband.

Welcome to the extranjero. You're on your own, man. Thank God this was not Grand Cayman Island. If some kid was feeling sick, he was keeping his nausea to himself. All the nausea in this place was of the existential sort—the kind that comes from realizing one is utterly ineffectual against the barriers that life puts our way—barriers like race, gender, class—and, yes, the condition of being born into this inexplicable world.

Someone had some advice for travelers. Throw out everything. If you can't perceive, you can't guide others to your perception. What makes you edgy is what is best. The idea of being locked in a prison, or kidnapped for some sort of ransom to be extracted from my parents is what made me edgy. I spoke Spanish and had been in South America, so that simultaneously took the edge off and added another dimension. That edge was bitter and grim and exhilarating like paranoia.

If I took any kind of trip, I generally tried to get straight with my inner self. Talk about a fruitless endeavor, what added up to a misspent youth. Besides, I finally concluded, isn't the state of psychic confusion what road-tripping's all about? Expanding consciousness and defamiliarizing yourself. I wanted to live the experiences of 18th-century English Lady Mary Wortley Montague, who traveled to the Ottoman Empire, dressed herself as a typical female resident and sneaked into the Turkish Baths incognito.

Because I spoke Spanish, I wanted to blend in. Try it all out without anyone pigeonholing me as an Ugly American. You'd never catch me bellowing out the *Star-Spangled Banner*. How self-immolating, though. Why erase my identity? What was the point? I should take up smoking. How many thousands of documents have been destroyed in the name of progress, love, poor judgment, material? American dream? Superwoman? Autonomous, self-engendering creature of the '90s?

It was all possible because I quit. I just walked out of the trendy gourmet coffee store I had opened up in my hometown city somewhere in a vast, happy place I tried to represent in all my store's flyers and brochures. It all took place somewhere else, though. Somewhere in that Great Pie-in-the-Sky blame-the-victim downsizing, outplacing, take-your-pay-cut-and-smile-you-still-have-a-job shopping mall I came to know as My Life.

And here I was in Paraguay.

Would I meet many other Americans in Paraguay? Argentina was running through my mind. When Evita Peron stopped dreaming, she began to die. Brains require dreams for our inconceivable consciousnesses. Cats dream. Predatory identifications.

Jorge Luis Borges, I've read quite a few of your books. My experience is focused in chromosomes and gene sequences. That means I have no choice.

I took a taxi to my hotel, the Hotel Asunción Palace, which had been the palace and residence of the 19th-century dictator Lopez. He had been in love with a daring Irish woman who came to be known as Madame Lynch. My room was on the second floor. I ascended the marble staircase, gripping the gorgeous wrought-iron railing.

The hallway of the old palace smelled of oranges and floor polish. I felt sweat roll down my back. "What is the purpose of propaganda in this town?" Promotion, man, promotion. And tomorrow they're having a Paraguayan cookout in my honor. It was called an asada. The event would have little or nothing to do with my "honor" and more to do with the people I happened to know.

Meaning—what does the "meaningful experience" bring to bear? Publication is important to all of us? Not so much. State of death represents the end of *Tibetan Book of the Dead*. "We" realize. "We" do this. "We" understand.

I really didn't give a shit if I didn't come back alive.

Smell of papaya. Reincarnation is different than transmigration of souls to resurrect the body. Mummy concepts occur over and over. Reincarnations can be taken for granted. Avoid if possible. Doubt the possibility of an afterlife. All-Americanisms & I'm working and fighting for something or another.

Two days later. There was now something to look forward to. Dinner with someone I had met earlier that day when I went to the airport to confirm my reservations and to pick up the luggage lost in the detour to Rio. Paraguay was starting to take on film noir edges. I had happened into his life in the airport while he was waving officials through Immigration and letting my baggage go unmolested through the Aduana (Customs).

The Aduana was to be feared in any South American country. Strange how I had already figured out that if someone needed help with luggage, all I needed to do was to tip fairly well, and voila!—no problem slipping through Customs with who-knows-what quantity of catalogues, brochures and samples. No commercial value. No dutiable goods. But still subject to Customs. The threat was something that hovered in the air like humidity in this sweaty place.

Here they eat a thick, fish stew to give strength. An aphrodisiac, like the way the light flickers on the wavecap in the river.

Immortality is a privilege of the truly rich. The unruly. The giant monument gives you hope, doesn't it. Run run run. You just can't control how your body gets plundered in this life or the next.

I heard someone talking in the dining room, while they drank coffee and read one of the five major daily newspapers of Asunción. "He died before the ambulance could reach him." "Qué pena." "Was it an accident?" "The commissioner says yes."

And who would ever question?

My mysterious new friend arrived exactly on time. He had a single rose to give me. I was startled. He didn't even know my full name and he was giving me red roses?

I could see my premonitions were eerily taking shape. I probably wouldn't get out of this country alive. For some reason, the idea didn't perturb me. It actually made me laugh.

After dinner in a lovely restaurant with a bouganvillia-lined patio, we returned to his green Mercedes. He made an announcement. "I'm going to meet my old boss—pay him a visit."

He had a pained expression on his face, so I half-expected a visit to the local cemetery. Was this a Paraguayan's idea of a date? "Where are we going?" I asked.

"It's near here. It's the prison," he said.

"What??" I thought I must have misunderstood.

"Prison. My boss was accused of something he didn't do," he said. "Do you mind?"

"Yes. I need to go back to the hotel. I'm tired," I said.

"Okay. Here we are. I'll take you back to the hotel soon."

The prison wasn't surrounded by barbed-wire and there was no guard tower. Nevertheless, it had an ominous presence. We walked to the front gate and my friend slipped the guard a 10,000 guarani note, about the equivalent of five dollars. Five bucks and you've got access to the prisons that Amnesty International would kill to enter. Kill, but don't torture.

Nervous, but intensely curious, I wished I had a small hidden camera. The place did not have the smell I expected it to have. I didn't hear screams. It was not musty—simply vaguely antiseptic.

"I enjoyed the book you gave me very much—it was very good." He was talking to someone.

"I'd like you to meet my wife," he said to the nephew of his imprisoned ex-boss. That was his way of introducing me.

"Your wife?" he asked. "Let me be the first to congratulate you."

Of course we weren't married. Hell, I had only met him two days before. So. An American wife had some sort of totemic pull around here. And who was I to question? I didn't have any guarani-notes to bribe my way out of this prison if I pissed off anyone.

The nephew accompanied us to his room. "He's not there." The knock on the door was ominous. It echoed like Argentina and the desaparecidos.

"No one's in the room," my friend repeated to me. Funny to call a cell a room. Funny to have a "room" in a Paraguayan prison. Funny to be not there.

"He must be at Mass."

"Oh."

It would never even go to trial. He did not give evidence. And trying to find the only one who knew the truth. He might have been just anybody.

Authority, its excesses, always turned me on. That was probably my worst problem.

"Wife?" I asked him in the car. "Why did you say that???"

"I wanted to fuck with his mind," he said.

"Well, you certainly fucked with mine," I said. He only laughed.

The next night we were eating surubai fish, caldo de pescado, at a river-front diner. Smiling, perched on a hard vinyl stool, leaning up next to him, laughing sweating in the interminable, ubiquitous humid skin. Love is something like this.

I wondered if it what the guys in the dining room had been talking about the other day was really an accident. What did it matter? His boss was still in prison. I was still incarcerated in my existential pain and grief. At least no one had died. Yet.

Once the breakthrough is made, there is a permanent expansion of awareness. We go kicking and screaming all the way.

"Por la razon o por la fuerza," he said.

"What are you talking about?" I asked.

"Truth," he said. "It's on every Chilean coin. By reason or by force."

Am I wrong? Wrung out? See things in a new way. Reconceive archetypes, clichés, eternal verities and breathe! Reconfigure perception. The word for DAWN in guarani refers also to a physical state—a condition of one's body. Warmth coming up over the self. Identity melting, softening up.

His smile was beautiful and warm. Within two days, I had fallen in love. Quickly thereafter, I had fallen down into my past and my self-preserving/self-imprisoning structures. Mind. Consciousness. Make me aware of what I know and what I don't know.

Look out the window—human perception—biting into freshly-baked chipas. Chipa with thick crust, chewy, warm, delicious interior.

"It is probably a sin to love you so much," he said.

Simultaneity. I was thinking of him, craving him, wanting him as a synchronous gesture, a movement in our bloodstreams, mixed up and all together.

"Es probablemente un pecado amarte tanto."

To hear it in Spanish bothered me even more. A sin. Un pecado. Compulsion would get you here in this dark, silent Paraguayan prison.

He said he was in love with me. I referred to him as my "friend," just to avoid details, but everyone was onto me.

But who was my mysterious friend? And then they had to flee the country by night. Death is at the bottom of everything. The Brazilian border was thick, hot and fearful, like everything in these calm, dangerous South American nights.

"His papers were forged," he said.

"Why bother? He was a public official. Didn't everyone know who he was?"

Smiling through the airport. When did I stop having the urge to run away. I wanted smiles and dollars. Anything you can do for me I'll appreciate.

Papers in order.

Bowl of "caldo de pescado" waiting for me at La Reina, the diner near the port.

The diesel exhaust coated my face, the washcloth was black with soot. I loved the shower with endless supplies of hot water. The water, warm & steamy, mixed with my sweat and made me aware of what I know and what I don't know.

There is no such thing as "should" in respect to art or music or literature.

No. I couldn't ask any more questions. The answers were too circular, to invented. And when I wanted answers, they spoke Guarani.

The wife had a packet of papers in her hands. The police officer was also a member of the secret militia group that no one claimed existed in this town.

The skin of the carved poultry was vitreous. Identity as erased in the shadows, reconstructed for the moment. "Disguises?" I asked.

"Soluciones," he said. His Spanish was still difficult for me to understand.

At the interrogation that began at the police station, the wife had interrupted. "You won't learn anything from them. They're only love letters. They're the only thing I have left."

During the Stroessner regime, they used to torture people at the police commissioner's headquarters. "O es conmigo o es mi contra," he used to say. "Whoever's not FOR me is AGAINST me."

I tried to communicate, but they were speaking Guarani. It's better not to be mixed up in things like this.

The house was under construction and had been for nine years. "We're tired already of the renovation," his mother had told me. I was in love with her son. She knew it. We all knew. Everyone but me.

A gun can make some real changes. Dogmatic ways of thinking are counterproductive for survival. We're at a terrible disadvantage.

And here I was with a falsified passport and no visa to Brazil. I had no way out. It would be stupid to lie. I had good friends I had never met. At least that's what they wanted me to believe.

All Paraguayan asadas had the same food—carne asada (beef prepared on an outdoor grill), sopa paraguaya (cornbread dressing, with onions), salchichas (sausages).

"You'll find the body in the police report," he said. I remembered the other night when he insisted upon going to a friend's house to watch *The Godfather*—dubbed in Spanish. *El Padrino*. I was surprised and somewhat alarmed to see that he had entire passages memorized.

"I've always dreamed of being a Godfather type."

"Oh cool." I tried to disguise my nervousness. Instead of commenting I coughed. I remember him saying to me that if he wanted me or anyone else detained, he could do it, and no American embassy could do anything but sit and watch.

I tried to sound indifferent, almost sardonic. "What 'business' would you have?—Dry cleaners? Gas stations? Prostitution? Porno movie houses? Cigarette vending machines?"

He looked at me quizzically.

"Or would you just be a hitman?" I asked. He laughed.

"Eres un peligro. You're trouble. You are a menace to society—you and your observations. Are you having fun fucking with me?" He was still laughing. I was pretending to be laughing. Perhaps he was pretending, too.

True madness occurs in disguise. Under the superficial veneer of polite warmth, protocol, and procedure, we could feel the presence of death, of cool, dead lips and haunting silence.

"I've got to visit someone," he said a week later.

"More friends in prison?" I asked.

"No. Worse. More permanent," he replied.

We went to a velatorio near the Avenida Mariscal Lopez, down the street from the Burger King and a place were street vendors sold a sweet drink made of sugar cane and honey.

I didn't know exactly what a velatorio was. I thought we were entering some sort of hotel or pension.

"Senora, un cafecito?" A uniformed waiter was carrying a tray of drinks.

"Si, como no," I said. I took a little espresso cup from the tray and sipped the warm, bitter liquid. It was sweetened.

Somehow it dawned on me that this was a wake. I tried to look appropriately sad, although I didn't know the victim or the family. The wake was for a 22-year-old law student killed in a car accident over Easter weekend.

Quiet. Reciting a rosary. "Mama!" someone called from the street. The mother burst into hysterical weeping. "I don't want to live! No puedo seguir viviendo. Quiero que me entierren con mi hijo! I want them to bury me with my son."

I walked into the other room where the mother was weeping in order to avoid looking indifferent. That was when I saw it. Coffin. Swollen face. Purple lips. Gray, purplish cheeks. Swollen hands. Purple fingernails. "Do you want to say a rosary?" No. No no no no no no.

And the fainting spell wasn't as easy to disguise as my nausea. "Is she all right? What's happening?"

Someone helped me out of the room. I started to recover a little of my balance but then I caught the odor of death. They say it's distinctive. It's not. It's just like armadillo, opossum, or any other thing you might run across on a summer day in south-central Texas.

"Do you believe, Senoñra, in the stream of consciousness?"

No. I think it's all a fake. Language makes the consciousness, not the other way around. So, it's a stream of language, not of "consciousness." Consciousness is something else. Consciousness is choice. Choosing a meaning-making process that suits you.

And who influenced you? And Mr. Jorge Luis Borges, where would you put him? In the labyrinth I've decided is a paradigm not for my mind but for my love life. Endless retracing of the same tired places, finding the minotaur in the middle who will always place me face to face with a false passport, a fake Rolex watch, and a leather valise of ñandutí, Paraguayan crochet.

Of course, the soul-destroying minotaur in the middle of the labyrinth is always oneself.

His face was shadowed and ominous in the darkness of dusk and wrought-iron work along the windows.

I started the interview with that image in my mind. They wanted to know what I would write about. They expected irony, sentimental views of women, and an evasion of true emotion. I gave them something truthful because I was fed up.

"It is prohibited for her to leave the country without my approval. I've already arranged it with Immigration." I laughed. No one else did.

Hours later, I woke up in his apartment, a cotton comforter tucked around my body, a soft pillow against my cheek.

The apartment was dark, with candles flickering in the cold South wind. He had lit candles because he said the light was softer and it would keep me from having nightmares. Too late, I thought to myself. When would he stop introducing me as his wife?

We made love in an apartment that had the shadows and whispers of the velatorio. Sex in a satin-lined bed, headboard etched with patterns like handwriting or eroded carvings on the face of a marble headstone.

"Why so desperate, mi amor?" I asked. I wanted to be far away from the smell of swollen, purple lips, hands bursting around the fingernails. "Why do you want to marry me so quickly?"

He didn't answer. Later, I had my own explanation: "There was some sort of time deadline. No doubt. Without funds, perhaps he'd end up in the Paraguayan prison with his ex-boss, the ex-president of the national port authority."

A few weeks later, I watched a reporter in a rumpled plaid shirt start an interview on television. He was talking to a French diplomat just returned from South America. "Is it true you were there just before Paraguay's experiment in democracy collapsed and they returned to a military dictatorship?"

"Yes. And no. Basically it is a difficult situation. A murder story based on fact. It started as a series of journal entries, and ended up as an heuristic—a self-uncovering of the mental structures that trap me to a certain number of explanations—or at least discourse possibilities."

I didn't realize until later that I had dreamed this.

"Look at it this way. I'm doing something dangerous. You were, like me, born to be murdered."

The reporter didn't much like that last remark. Perhaps that was what woke me from my dream.

"You live until you die, so you've gotta do something, right?— Listen to these elements; the ex-president of the port being framed for drug smuggling, my "fiancee" pushing me for a quick marriage, the best friend selling used cars, the friend preparing exit visas for the tortured ones shoved into the river. But that was 20 years ago. He stilled himself and played out the exigencies of the culture."

"I might as well become a missionary," I said. In my dream, I was talking to the French diplomat and the reporter.

"Are there many missionaries in Paraguay?" he asked. It was something he could understand.

"Yes. They start a lot of schools and medical clinics," I said. "And then there's the Peace Corps."

Lights in the square accentuated shadows. English was becoming a problem for her after spending so much time staring into the tear-stained space she once called a window, or a mirror.

Rain. Rain, rain, and more rain. March 21 meant the first day of autumn, but today the storms were like springtime, with drops smearing each pane of glass, each unbearable stretch of venetian door opening to the outside.

Paraguay. Smuggler's paradise. Stealing medicines. Selling out-dated, fraudulent goods. Insurance companies were studying the technique to see if they could incorporate it into their HMOs. A missionary clinic—that was what made it even worse. Combining the corporal and the spiritual had never been so painful.

My conditioning was unshakable. It kept coming up in my future events as well as my past. Humiliated, frustrated reason. 20th-century preoccupations coming to a head in the backwaters of a Paraguayan river, a deranged parrot screaming obscenities and overheard confessions. Big green parrot of the torture room.

And still I smelled death clinging to the hairs of my arm, the folds of my eyelids. Seeing through eyes brought down by death. "That parrot wants to bite me," I complained.

It was daylight and we were sitting in a garden confiteria eating pastries and drinking cafe con leche.

"Ja, ja, ja," he said, in the Spanish-language equivalent to "You've gotta be fucking kidding me."

"I think you've got something in mind for me and I'm nervous," I said to him. I said it in English to see what would happen.

"If you help me, I'm prepared to help you. Asunción is a closed city, Miss Smith. You can't get out." He looked at me with amusement.

"Don't toy with me, man," I said. I pretended to be playful. It was terrifying.

Evolution is not reversible. I can't get my shame back.

Standing on the edge of the balcony, looking down upon the rubble left by war and unreasonable celebrations. The stunning sky was madness embodied. Childhood ropes and uniforms left abandoned with carousels, and all with a stasis we came to see as surrealism when it was 8000 km away, but as authoritarianism when too near.

"I want to talk to the ghost of Orson Welles." It was all I could think of to say after the awkward silence that followed. The reporters would have preferred I speak of Maria Bemburg or Agosto Roa Bastos.

Next day. He drove his Mercedes up to the guard station at the Port. I was restless and edgy. I shouldn't have called my office. They were wiring me money I didn't want.

Don't call your old boyfriends "victims." That was one of the first rules things I learned. I chose not to put my lesson into practice.

"Where are we?"

"The port. Where I work. I want you to see something," he said.

"Are we going to be here long?" I asked.

"I need to inspire the workers," he said. It was the eve of a major strike. "We've lost ground here. Morale. No joking around."

"Who jokes about starvation?"

I used to believe in God. I still do, but my sense is that God helps me make peace with inevitability. I wish you'd brought me antacids from home. I'll meet you any time any place. You remember that.

Enlightened interdependence. However, by the inexorable vampiric existence. They all take more than they need. Avoid trouble for yourself. Don't let it rub off on you.

He jumped out of the car, whipped off his belt and began to whip the guards.

Produce peace. The cuckoo clock. Chocolates. Dairy products. We expect too much. Fruits and wood in the ships. Don't ask what is in the containers.

Someone switched my real passport with a fraudulent one.

There are some mistakes too egregious to ever turn over in my mind. I make mistakes. Don't wallow.

I want to meet Orson Welles. I want to talk to his spirit. I want the mad scramble to innovate, juxtapose image against image, break the mind in clouds of steam, darkness, light.

River flowing slowly over the nests of ducks, crocodiles, trash washed up after the last flood. Motifs of rescue.

Two weeks later.

Splash of people swimming in the hot springs in the hills near Paraguari, 75 miles north of Asunción.

We went there in search of stretch of river with rapids. Dirt road, lots of dust. A cabin. Clothesline stretched out in back, dirt yard beaten down. Three guys drunk on cheap rum running out to charge us

20,000 guaranis to go to the river. "But isn't it government property?"
They happened to be living in an abandoned farmhouse on the
way. One guy throwing himself under the axle, squealing. The others
perhaps brandishing guns.

This would have been a great scene for a western. In fact, some-
one had made a Paraguayan version of a spaghetti western here. The
Paraguayan werewolf hunter wore a Clint Eastwood poncho and
talked of his solitary life. We laughed and we didn't know why.

Film is just another medium. Falsify my rights. I still have illusions,
dreams, and something else. Paraguay has the feel of a noir film, with
deranged tangos and danger around each sweet, dark note. The beau-
tiful harp played *Noches Paraguayas* and other polkas used not only in
love but also in battle.

The phone rings. Cell phone. Digital pager, called "beepers." Sur-
rounded by broad-leaf trees and flowering plants. Let us all do what
is expected. The Mercedes had leather seats and the smell of his
cologne. We loved each other almost too much. I knew what to ex-
pect even before it happened.

"Do you like it? This is the house my grandfather built."

Of course, under his guidance, the place was a wreck. It was a
massive, stucco-concrete affair that had been originally conceived of
as a two-story Spanish colonial affair, but now was a nightmare of
scaffolding, piles of sand, and improbably small and ineffectual tools.

"The worse thing is that with all the construction, there have
been absolute SWARMS of cockroaches. Oh, and would you like
another cheese sandwich?" He offered me a plate with a few scraps
of sandwich in the middle.

"Uh. No. Thank you," I said.

I looked down, discreetly I hoped, and sure enough, there was a
cockroach lying dead by my foot, almost the size of the six-inch
Chaco grasshoppers I had seen the week before.

"You know, with your interest in film making, you could do a
great movie here—a Tennessee Williams play adopted for film. Or
Borges, of course," I said, trying to get my mind off the cockroach
menace.

"Did you know these walls are two feet thick?" he said.

"Why?"

"They're solid."

"I don't doubt that."

"Today's houses have flimsy, hollow walls," he said.

"Well, at least you have a place to route the wiring and the telephone lines," I said. The only light in the room came from a single bulb hanging from a thin chain suspended from the ceiling. There was a plastic garden chair in the living room, another lawn chair draped with a blanket in front of the television. I felt very uncomfortable to see the poverty he tried so hard to mask.

"When do you think it will be finished?" I asked.

"It depends." He led me to the courtyard where the swimming pool had been drained, the water replaced by building materials.

"Well, at least there's a lot of sand for your son—he can build a lot of sandcastles."

The governor of my own state back in the U.S. had referred to our economy as being Third World. Perhaps he was trying to inspire us to try harder. Were there homes like this there? Grand and imposing from the street, but a decrepit wreck inside?

Undoubtedly.

And there we were, in the shadow of the poshest most elaborate shopping mall in all of Paraguay. Grammars are complicated. Dogs chase predetermined oblivions. The breeze made the bare bulb tremble and swing on its chain. Where are we going? The car tires made a distinctive noise traveling down the cobbled roads. It is a set of symbols that could be arranged in a new way.

Cross. Tombstone. Graves. English heritage. A child coming into focus. Purchasing lace, earrings, hand-tooled leather, and sadness.

The pillars were pink, new the actual facts of perception. I was being cut by random factors. All things are happening at the same time, but only because we see things in a certain way, we decide to make it line up so that it seems linear. The flicker of candles in the apartment as we made love. Smell of oranges and sound of the night breeze through the thick, flower-laden leafy trees.

His mother could have been my grandmother. There was an odd resemblance. His great-grandfather was English. The tombstone said "Boston, England." I suspected they had made a mistake, and they meant "Boston, New England." Who knows. How many Americans in the 19th century tried to pass themselves off as English?

Enemy if I am you. Sound of engine firing up. Cafe con leche.

Sweetened coffee, pastries. Sitting in the apartment, listening to pop music from Spain. Characteristic voices, characteristic accents. Good. Sweating, sleeping together.

When did you stop wanting to move to South America?

Never.

Do you think you'll get out alive?

N   e   v   e   r.

Doomsday Belly

I. In my idea of a perfect world, I would be a model son, and you would be my model parents. You would do what I wanted.

But, this is no perfect world.

You're not my dad. He's dead. At least, that's what they told me when I got out of the hospital after my last suicide attempt—the one where I tried to enema myself to death with hot buttered rum while reading Baudrillard's *Fatal Strategies*. But, that's another story. For this one, I promised I wouldn't mix postmodernist intellectual icons with the gritty, sweaty, ass-clenchings of an ugly kid from an ugly, cheap, suburban wanna-be place.

They tell me Dad's dead. Too bad. While he was alive, he was the original maverick over-the-top, semi-suicidal, semi-Parnassian, bolt-of-lightning-to-the-head, awe-inspiring entrepreneur worth $1 million bucks this week, not worth a kick in the scrotum-sac the next. Local newspapers and business 'zines loved to put his smarmy, toothy, grifter grin on their covers. They would interview him & he'd talk about his work, his life, his new cabin in Montana. He never mentioned me.

But, why should he?

I should know it all by now—especially now I've become my own Dad—only in a matter of speaking, of course. I think, therefore I heave. Bitter tears while dark sky inverting under black plastic cups held under bathroom spigots and mouth drooling with the nausea of *Phaedrus* realizing transcendence is only another form of rejection. I'm telling you, the voice never got any nicer—"You're FAT! You're SOFT! You spend too much time in front of that DAMN TV! Don't eat so many GREASY TACOS!"

Not likely.

"Good God, you make me sick. Look at you. So fat I can't tell if you're a boy or a girl!"

I started wearing T-shirts that hung down to my knees. What could I do to not be me? My shadow on the sidewalk was like an ink tide on the white granite shoreline during a full moon in Maine.

My shame made me sweat. I would have kissed a ragged sock if it had come from the foot of someone who cared.

It was my body, of course. My forearms were cotton seizing up with every baptism of steamy, salty sobs. I tried to bleach the stains, but my sins could never know redemption. I only called them sins because I had no other vocabulary. If I had more time and more energy, I would rename "Sin" and call it by its functional name—something like "STAPLE GUN" or "AIRLINE BAGGAGE HANDLING SYSTEM"—anything to communicate the mangling, mutilating, immobilizing power of that single word.

For me, SIN began and ended with the body. My sin and my body were synonymous. Bad joke, but true enough.

I should never have been born in this impossible body—my father could see through to the dark black echo where my heart should have pounded rebellion and a long, fat smear of toothpaste over the mirror.

Sartre would have been proud. I had disconnected identity with image. My face in the mirror was not my heart on my sleeve. What fogged up my windows on a cold, gray morning was a nothingness that imitated the existential anxieties of men and women facing certain death by plague.

What will be the new psychobabble word for "denial"? Tweezer? It fits, doesn't it. Tweezer. Something you use to pluck and shape and sculpt, but it's not radical enough to get rid of the thing. The eyebrows will always grow back. But still you pluck. And still you deny. You're in a state of "Tweezer," baby, now hand me a fresh razor.

If I could construct a utopian society, no one would be a zit on someone else's ass. Every person would have a place, and everyone would be appreciated for her or his unique beauty.

This is not what happened to me. The story of my life is simple. I reached puberty. I went to college. My voice faded like a silk screen put through too many washings. What I wanted was a gold-plated falsetto when I wept alone, driving home. What I got was a hoarse, snuffling gurgling that sounded like I had just inhaled the foam from a fresh decaf latté at the Jamaica-Side Coffee House.

I could only cry decently after a box of amaretto biscuits, a vacuum-packed tin of beef jerky, and a round of Sir Thomas More's *Utopia*, followed by Wilhelm Reich's early essays on the origins and implications of sexual repression.

The last book I read said I could blame everything on alien abduction and repressed memories. But, that won't work. They've got it backwards. Aliens did not abduct me—I'm an alien who was abducted by humans—not all humans, but one. I still dream in my native tongue—I hear and speak in the low whistles, whines, and vowelless spackle of my original alien language.

The worst summer was the summer I ended up in the Carson City, Nevada Community Hospital Nut Ward. They called it Generalized Anxiety. I called it "Life With Dad-the-Nuts-out-Nevada-Necrophile." It was the summer he hired me to drill for gold. It wasn't pretty to be out there, if you ask me. The Earth-Rape he called "Exploratory Drilling" left a scar in the desert that would take about 2,000 years of dust storms, flash floods, and mustang trampling to erase.

Can you imagine the hell it was for me? He divorced my mom while she was in the middle of chemotherapy because he said that women in wigs just didn't turn him on. That didn't make sense, though. The women I saw him with in Nevada had Big BIG Hair.

I was willing to try. I went to FloraLee's Wig Shop and bought the biggest, blondest, Dolly Partonesque wig you could imagine. Then I bought some silver strappy high heels and a fuschia lycra mini-skirt and tube top. It's what I wore to work one morning I was sure old Big Hair Dad would show up. Sure enough, there he came, in a cloud of playa lake-bed dust kicked up by his decade-old Range Rover.

That old fuck. I wanted him to love me, even though I hated him.

The first time I dressed up in women's clothes for Dad's benefit was when I was 13. I won't call it drag because I was not the least bit camp about it—I believed in what I was doing—I thought I wanted to win against my mother once and for all. But, of course, it was a vicious parody of all those Apple-Pie-&-Pass-the-Prunes values. Imagine, those coat-hanger eyes.

Dad came home from the airport, and there I was in full lycra regalia. I was fat. The lycra was wet with armpit sweat and greasy, tomato-y stains from the lasagna I had dripped on it.

I wanted him to look at me & realize that Mom was no different. Women are ugly, I said. Women sweat under their arms and they spill sauce on their clothes. They will embarrass you.

Hate her. Love me. It was that simple.

Dad didn't see it that way. Or, if he did, he mixed it up.

Hate me. Love her. It was easier like that. He'd lose a son, but gain a few contracts from confidants he bitched to about me.

Love is never saying you are spit and grease in the morning. My love is like a red, red rose-shaped blob of vomit or hairball on the carpet. Love and a hairball. They're the same thing—disgusting, even though natural processes.

He said, "Never—I mean NEVER—let me catch you wearing ANYTHING like this." But, I had already changed back to my Dress-for-Success suit and tie, so I didn't know what he was talking about.

He must have been confused.

Bite the weak. Maim the sick. Gouge the eyes from the artists, shove pointed sticks in the ears of the musicians, break the fingers of the poets and sappy utopians. I love the smell of memory.

II. They told me I was a male child. They called me their son.

Why didn't they ever tell me the truth? Being part of the great circus called MALE GENDER meant having a penis. I didn't have one. They told me that since I was a premature baby, some parts of me hadn't grown in yet. I guess that included my penis, and, if they expected me to believe them (which I did), part of my BRAIN.

The man with no penis and half a brain.

No wonder Dad was ashamed of me. No wonder my mom left. No wonder I began compulsively overeating to fill the gnawing void in the pit of my belly—the place I pointed to as my heart.

I saved the little metal keys on the Spam cans and tied them to the laces in my boots. I threw the razor-sharp Spam cans into the backyards of people who had dogs that had tried to bite me. I drank the clear, pulpy, gelatinous goo from the bottom of the Vienna Sausage cans and thought of pigs getting their throats slit.

It was a pig-eat-pig world & I was queen/king of the swine. String me up by my cloven hooves, baby. Water the unsprouted penis bud that was somewhere within me. Spray weedkiller on my brain.

And still, there was Dad, Range-Rovering around the Nevada desert, hoping to find gold or have some excuse to dig a kick-ass pit the size of the one at Yerington that would fill up with the bluest, most toxic water you've ever seen in your life.

But, Dad's dead. The Dad I'm talking about could never have been my real dad, anyway. What I'm talking about is more like a Patriarchal Composite Dad-head of Psycho-mythological world. It's no closer to painting the picture of a real individual than are Karen Horney's sketches of feminine neurotic personalities.

Dad was a desert rat. He couldn't see his ratness. He didn't know he was wandering the desert like a guy split off from the tribes of Israel and the Promised Land.

And I was his son, he said. But I was split off from my gender and I had no hope of entering into the Kingdom of Sexual Certainty.

Would it help if I didn't hate Dad? Would it help if I didn't hate myself? You can guess the answer to those questions—I only remember the time I tried to cut all the carbohydrates and fat out of my diet so I'd be complete muscle & sinew over bone. I wanted to see what kind of shape I'd have. Would I still have big, sloppy, soft pectorals? Would I still have a wide, flat ass? Would I still have jowls?

I never found out.

The pressure of having no carbohydrates or sweets made me eat six tins of Argentinean corned beef and Hormel tinned meat product at a sitting. I hate meat. Why did I eat it? Ask a cannibal. It was an act of appropriation. Could I simply eat the attributes I wanted for myself? I revered the slaughter—the way the animals faced death. I wanted to taste their death hormones. I wanted to swallow their fear. I wanted to get ready for my own end. Tin me up in my coffin, but what will you put on my label? I have a name, but that doesn't begin to say who I am.

Dad's a modern-day Lost Man. He's no Victorian, but I can see him going from encampment to encampment, pretending to be mapping, but really simply running from the limited self they had back home. In the desert they can be as expansive and grandiose as they want. They can also be invisible. No one can find them. No one can get them.

When the moon is full, all the craters are visible.

Had he seen the desert as a place where you dig for food and you sniff out sex where you can get it?

"It's like drilling," I told Dad the last afternoon we were together. We were in Nevada, driving near American Barrick's Goldstrike operation. "Pure sex—no hope of pleasure. If it's beautiful it's because it's violent."

He looked out the window without blinking. "I feel sorry for your mother. And for me. But I don't know why. And I don't know why I don't know. I just don't know anything."

Maybe those weren't his exact words. Does it matter?

Dad's dead & I'm not going back to the hospital, no matter what happens.

The sunset was caustic but meaningless that night, like ammonia fumes on diamond chips. The sun set on iron. The moon rose slippery on a large, blank bowl of oil.

III. One night I woke myself up at 3 A.M. screaming. "The Bunch! The Bunch!" I had dreamed I was the entire Brady Bunch all balled up in one body. I had pigtails, bellbottoms, a Father-Knows-Best voice, an eggbeater in my hand, and I couldn't decide whether I wanted to be a junior-high cheerleader, a budding entrepreneur, or an incestuous touchy-feely stepmom figure. At least I wore sensible shoes.

When I got up, I discovered my toenails had been painted a light, pearlescent shade of pink.

I wasn't the scrappy little hockey player Dad was. I wasn't from Brunswick, Vermont, and I didn't join the Merchant Marines the minute I got out of high school. Dad said he thrived on hazings, initiations, and rites of passage. He said he liked eating shit when crossing the equator.

The truth was, Dad got off easy because the ship happened to have passengers each time he crossed the equator. Passengers meant potential witnesses. So, Dad just heard the stories. Perhaps stories of hazings were simply a part of a utopian theory—an experiment never carried out.

The Marquis de Sade was just another loony guy scribbling page after page after page of language that comes straight from the brain— no sanitizing middle loop to go through—it's just a straight download from right-brain, left-brain, half-brain.

Aren't they the same thing? Religious mania and sexual mania?

It's a linguistic convention that we have that makes them differentiated at all. In the end, all the commandments are the same.

THOU SHALT pluck out the weird, the weak, the faint of heart. If that wasn't on the *Dead Sea Scrolls* or in the early Nicene writings, it should have been.

My own flesh is as pallid as lust. It glimmers like polished ivory in the pale streetlight illumination that streams in my bedroom window. My flesh's high fat content makes me alabaster. I can be carved like soap with a wet saw. My sadness makes me glow.

Roman bronze masks from the Second Century A.D. reflect the pain of being a man. Gender will hurt you when the myths catch up to the fiber covering your eyes.

Dad told me the same stories over and over. I hated hearing them, and I think Dad knew it, but he wouldn't stop, and I couldn't seem to get up the courage to tell him to shut up—I already knew too much about man's inhumanity to men & women, and how people like to masquerade as gods in the face of the weak, the sad, the lonely, the self-reproaching.

I have never been touched in love or in any other expression of tenderness. Love is a check. Love is cash. Love is a tax dodge.

Mine arrived like clockwork every month in the mail. I treated the computer generated check like a love note or a birthday card. It wasn't. I was Dad's little write-off. Still, I liked that Christmas, birthday, bar-mitzvah, christening, graduation, and shower present all rolled up together and sent to me every month by Big Daddy—the Great Tooth & Cavity Fairy in the Sky.

I was a write-off in every sense of the word.

I should never have been born into this puffy, soft body—my mother's only legacy to me. Its refusal to harden into defined muscle taunted me with a mother I couldn't really remember. When a face appeared in my memory, I knew it was wrong—it was some sort of composite I had constructed from catalogues, fashion magazines and religious icons. I have no idea what kind of relation it bore to reality. My own sense of self was the same kind of composite—something I had either constructed myself or had been delivered to me by Dad.

Dad told me I was his son.

What happens when you find you're not? What do I do now that I don't think I'm a member of that gender at all?

IV. My mother left when I was 14 months old. Most of my life, I had no idea she was alive. I thought she had died.

For a while, I thought I'd become an architect, and I'd design the perfect house and the buildings for a perfect community. The houses were solar-heated, there were gardens, parks, and fountains. Murals were everywhere—between houses, on walls, on fences. I designed it after Tommaso Campanella's *La Città del Sole*—the murals were illustrations from a book of knowledge. Like Campanella, I wanted to illustrate science—the science of identity and forgiveness. But, I couldn't think of how to do it, so each wall was a blank.

It didn't mean anything to me any more.

Tearing down the model city was as creative as the original act. Couldn't complete annihilation of a corrupt world be as utopian an impulse as building a world of total control, where the oldest and most stubborn fathers called the shots? A water well drilled into brass and brocade twisted the fabric of Reason until it curled in on itself like two actors kissing on-screen. My hands were cavalcades of sadness and sleet. My windows would not open except in the collisions of night and decay. My father's smile was a spotlight on a catacomb wall. All he illuminated was death. My lips were nothing but highways that doomed you to travel around and around the words that spewed forth from a yawning, opened grave. My dawns were funereal and weak. I could no longer even begin to construct a model of a perfect world. It was no longer within me.

Finally, I tore it all down.

V. For the next year, I tried to teach myself Mayan hieroglyphics and art techniques. I made a plaster of paris human skull, painted it black, and inlaid it with turquoise, black onyx, and garnet. In the eye sockets I placed two green neon tornados. For teeth, I glued in dead rosebuds.

When I was 20, I found out—in the worst possible way, that my mother was alive. She called me up, told me she was down on her luck, and asked if I could loan her some money and put her up for awhile. I didn't have any money, but I didn't want her to suspect—I would use any pretext.

At that point, I would say anything to get her to take me back.

Didn't she know I just wanted to talk to her—to get to know her? The light of maternity is neon and quick and pink like a hangover. The antidote is a jalapeño sucked dry. The remedy is prayer sobbed into a steamy, soapy shower. Why did she throw me away?

She said she'd meet me at the Denny's near I-10 and El Centro Blvd., so I went there as fast as I could. I waited in front next to the dessert case with meringues, Boston cream pies, brownies, apple crisp, and peach cobbler, but no one showed up.

To ease the tension, I read the labels of the desserts aloud, and tried to recite the ingredients, and the recipes by heart. I kept my voice soft, and—I thought—discreet, but after about twenty minutes, people were beginning to stare. One girl in particular—a pimply, oily-faced blonde wearing a sweatshirt that read "PASSENGER SIDE AIRBAG"—kept curling her lip, snickering, and nudging her friend.

I looked at her face rather pointedly and raised my voice so she wouldn't fail to hear me. "CLEARASIL WORKS! TRY SOME!" I shouted. She huddled with her friend, who looked up. I grabbed my crotch, even though I knew there was nothing there. That made the joke even better. "OXY-CUTE THEM!" I said, this time a little louder. They didn't know there were no little bags of pus or otherwise gooey, sticky liquid to get rid of. She flinched and ducked, as if I had two big zits in my hand, squeezing them so that the puss would hit her full in the face.

The assistant manager I knew as "Hello, My name is WAUKITA JO" watched part of this piece of performance art, and came rushing up to either seat me or swish me out the door. I tried to look studious and analytical. I pretended to have been debating the relative merits of Denny's preservative-laden pies, shipped frozen from the wholesaler.

"Can I help you?" asked Waukita Jo.

"French Silk," I said. The way I said it made it sound like a cheap porno film title or the brand name of a line of Made-In-Haiti lingerie. Believe it or not, it was the name of a pie.

"What?" She looked suspicious, but then her face changed. She had decided I was drunk.

"One piece. With coffee. For here," I said. "But, maybe you should seat me first. Then I'll give you my order."

"Oh, yes, of course." She looked at me a little uncertainly, then added an anarchistic little "sir."

On the TV above the take-out counter, a couple of preachers were describing the evils of legalizing brothels. They had films, and they interviewed a haggard, drug-addicted whore. Her body screamed for redemption. I said a prayer for her. Not for her sins, but for her humiliation. What were they paying her to tell her story? They acted like they were listening. Wasn't that the cruelest kind of lie?

The waitress brought me what I had ordered. It looked clean. A thin woman, who held her vestiges of beauty around her like a ragged version of the Bayeux tapestry draped over a castle wall, walked into Denny's. If she was my mother, she wasn't letting me know.

Raising myself up out of my aqua vinyl booth seat, I got a better look at her. I decided she might be the one. I'd keep my eye on her.

I ate my French Silk pie and drank the WE MAKE IT FRESH FOR YOU AT DENNY'S coffee. It occurred to me that maybe my mother was too ashamed to meet. Perhaps she didn't want to have to deal with the enormity of her guilt. Perhaps she, too, was suffering from a state beyond redemption. Perhaps she should never have been born into her impossible body, because female was not the gender she was cut out to deal with.

Talk about a sad situation.

There were too many ambiguities, and being female meant there were consequences for every action—being a woman involved dire consequences much beyond the imaginings of any male.

Pregnancy, for one. It's different for a woman than for a man. A man can see pregnancy, touch the belly, and fall down in awe in the spectacle of sprouting life, but can he really feel what it means to be pregnant? Once, I talked to a pregnant woman at the pool who had just finished swimming laps. She looked like hell. Big varicose veins, and stretch marks. Poor woman, I thought. Her husband is probably lusting after other women while she carries his child.

She seemed happy enough, though.

Swimming kept her from getting elephant ankles, she said.

How about backaches? I asked. Well, yes, it helped with that, too. How about with heartache, betrayal, rejection, denial? How about with being kicked in the gut? Getting thrown away? I didn't ask her those last questions. With her standing there bulging, I could feel an uncomfortable warmth in my swimsuit. I ducked into the men's locker room.

Just thinking about it was making my face flush. The waitress who was warming up my coffee looked at me oddly. "You okay? Need anything else, hon?"

I mopped my forehead with a napkin. Across the crowded dining room, the pimply-faced girl, who was now paying her check, glared at me with open hostility. I looked up at the waitress. "My name is not HON," I said. "It's SWEETIE-PIE. But you can call me AL-DOUS, or MR. HUXLEY."

"Geez. Don't have a cow," she said. I decided to give her a better than decent tip. She lacked a sense of humor, but she had a nice little belly.

I returned to my daydreaming. After I had talked to the pregnant woman at the pool, I strapped to my stomach an inflatable camping pillow which I had filled with water. I wanted to see what it would feel like to walk around with a big pregnant weight on my gut. Within two hours, I had a backache. The breasts swell, too, I remembered. So, I strapped on two 5-pound water balloons. The experience left me with a pulled shoulder muscle and a lower back pain that would make a grown man squeal like a pig. War is hell.

The haggard woman I had observed coming into Denny's was handing the cashier some money. As she exited the restaurant for the parking lot, I bolted out of my seat to catch her before she drove off into the cold, dark neverland of abandonment. The way she never even looked back into Denny's convinced me that she was indeed my mother.

It was cold in the parking lot. My veins were as rigid and intractable as diesel exhaust compressed into a bicycle tire. My eyes were thick with hope.

"Mom! Mom!" She didn't turn around. I thought I'd try a new approach, a new form of address. "Mother!"

The sound of engines backfiring made a melted liquid memory of my brain. The act of going away was a gunshot into the sunset. She wasn't going to stop.

"Mother! I'm here. I got your call. You can stay with me. I've got money."

Up close, she wasn't as ragged and down on her luck as she had seemed when I first saw her in Denny's. Her sweater was one of those hand-knitted novelty sweaters festooned with hearts, doves, and satin ribbons. Her earrings were long, dangly ropes of baroque pearls. Her perfume was Marcella Borghese's *Il Bacio*. She was driving a gold Lexus. She didn't need money, that was for sure. Something must have been bothering her, though, to call me.

"Mom, are you pregnant again?"

The woman, who had previously not even looked at me, spun on her little pointy-toed Italian tasseled loafers.

"Are you talking to me? You get back from me or I'll shoot you with pepper spray! I've really got some."

"Mom, please don't be mean to me. You called me and I'm here. I'm your son, Kristian. I'll help you."

The Denny's sign made a halo around her head. Her face had that same scouring searchlight look Joseph in search of a clean, well-lighted bale of hay he could shred so his wife could calve. Did the madonna know the implications of being a madonna right away, or did she have to wait until her son was dead?

"Are you out of your mind? I'm not your mother! How could I be? Take a look at yourself. You're no son of mine! You're a white boy!"

That was something I hadn't considered. She had a point. It didn't make me feel any less bitter, or any less abandoned.

"I'm sorry, ma'am." I shuffled back to Denny's, where my waitress was running toward me brandishing the check in her hand.

The woman got out her pepper spray and squirted some in my direction. "Now, don't you come following me!"

I watched the taillights of her Lexus disappear in the direction of I–10, and then I trudged back into the restaurant. I had lost my appetite, but I still had a restless, gnawing sensation inside my gut—not hunger, exactly, but something I couldn't push out of myself.

"Was that the person you were waiting for?" asked the waitress. Perhaps she felt sorry for me. I hated the fact that she was only pretending to listen—that she was just working me over for a good tip. While I pretended to sip on coffee, I slipped my hand beneath the table and pretended to jerk off into a paper napkin. Then I placed the napkin on the table, and stuck a $5 bill on top. That was her tip. One was worth something, the other was worth very little. She would spend the wrong one.

VI. In my own utopian world, mothers stay with their sons. If they leave, they take their sons with them. They don't leave them with a father whose best years were in the Merchant Marines, who does nothing but repeat the same anecdote until your memorized version of it is clearer and more lucid than his pathetic re-tellings of it.

You and I know his story is a lie.

Dad's not even my dad. Dad is a cultural composite.

This is the litany: Torture & terrorize the weak (forgetting that everyone is in fact weak). Make the act of denying your own mortality a moment of teeth-grinding fun. Cross entire oceans while ignoring your own need for the oceanic. Re-enlist in the Merchant Marines. Find a lover and write every day that you crave closeness. Sail away while you make your professions of love. Hurt people when the paradox is catching up to you. Tell no one your secret— that you encourage their bodies to get into you, but you don't know how to say NO. Don't let anyone see you cry. Live your life numb. Avoid them when you think they're becoming angry with you. Live in hopes of the next sleazy port. Maybe things will be different there. Maybe not. Maybe that cruel streak is something that can't be avoided, and you know it. You want to be hurt the next time you cross the equator. You pray there will be no passengers. Then you're afraid you'll fall in love. You pray for passengers.

After awhile I began believing that I had once been in the Merchant Marines. Me, on a beautiful little *Ship of Fools* memorialized by Hieronymous Bosch. Is this how I could start? Back up. Make it an anatomy lesson. A cold, sterile anatomy lesson where no one comes away with anything except confusion.

VII. The waters of the River Styx are blue, not black. Its depths team with air pockets and denial. I can't breathe when I think this way. I'll find my mother. I know I will. It will just take time. My eyes reflect the sky and that final journey from flesh to earth.

My mother paid for my sin—my sin of existence. I exist. That is my sin. Is this something I know, or is it something I see in the walls of my city which contain the illustrations of an age? I'll find my mother, and I'll ask her. Will she know the answers? In a perfect world, we would have perfect knowledge, and we would understand even the most flawed and broken mind. I'll find my mother.

People hurt me. People who don't even know me sense that I'm confused about my gender. That makes them hate me, but I don't know why.

It has happened so often that it's like clockwork—my body knows before my mind perceives it that it's going to happen again. I tell myself that I don't even mind it any more. Still, I understand that primitive urge to hurt the weak—but, since I am invariably the weak one, I don't know if it means I've internalized the urge and I won't be able to resist hurting myself.

If you don't want to be left out in the dark, you have to get ready to be hurt. That's just the way it is. Get ready. It's one more preparation for the death hormones. Eat meat. Don't eat meat. Swallow your own blood. Don't let your tears escape, but suck them back inside and swallow them, too.

Maybe they'll make you pregnant.

Babe in Arms

Life in the militia was not easy. Especially since Traynor, a woman, had decided to join up as a man. It was all a part of her "It's Not So Tough To Be a Tough Guy" experiment.

She was beginning to change her mind. It was tough to be a tough guy, and for all the wrong reasons. It wasn't because of the strength of mind, body, and spirit required. It wasn't because of the need for specialized knowledge of guns & ammo. Being a tough guy was tough because of the hideous tingling of buttcheeks falling asleep and the acrid, sour taste of drool oozing out the side of one's sagging lips, suddenly gone narcoleptic in the claustrophobic press of patriots sweating and straining to get in the last word.

Back in the good old days, when Traynor was still content to wear pantyhose and act docile as she fantasized about stirring arsenic into her locally famous Tex-Mex casserole, she had cross-stitched THE STATE OF NATURE IS ONE OF WAR into an Aida cloth banner. She framed it and put it over the sofa where HOME SWEET HOME used to be.

She was going to put a bumper sticker on her car—FREE SPEECH COSTS—but she decided the black helicopters would spot it. They'd have her number, and wouldn't she be sorry once the death camps were finished.

They wouldn't be able to tell that her camouflage haute-couture "doing the ultra-violent" stance was a farce, a mockery, a cabaret act.

She found the perfect la-cage-aux-militaires look at the Army Surplus store. Her favorite piece of the ensemble was the dirt-colored all-cotton boxer shorts. Imagining that a Gulf War veteran had probably worn similar undergarments without changing them for months made her feel a little weak-kneed. Ah, the selfishness, the tyranny, the crime embodied in a war-monger's boxers.

Life in the militia promised to be a place where tough, potent genitalia strained the elastic, where months of doing without made them slobber embarrassingly weak things about the loves of their lives—women who didn't even know they existed.

Her goal was to make someone fall in love with her, then mess with his head when he thought he had fallen in love with another man.

Her web would be as invisible as possible: she planned to exude as much feminine toxin as she could without blowing her cover. She wasn't going for the gay men. She wanted to seduce the straight ones. She wanted them to fall for him/her, torment themselves with their own libido, then lash out at themselves. She was looking forward to the drunken rages, the fistfights, the howls of pain and deception.

If she couldn't inspire love, at least she could inspire self-mutilation.

The actual day-to-day of the militia was a big disappointment. She had no idea militia meetings would be so boring. She had hoped for perversion and the occasional snake-bite ritual, but instead of draping their arms with rattlesnakes and jumping to Appalachian gospel music, these guys sat around and cleaned their guns. "Be sure to shine up the barrel of that thing," she said to LeRoy, who replied, "Yeah, okay," without any awareness whatsoever of the lewd intention behind her remark.

Where were the practice suicide rituals? Where was the vat of grape Koolaid or the little yellow cyanide pills passed out with the three Bs—beans, boots, and bullets?

LeRoy was standing in the hallway. Traynor could hear his high-pitched monotone. "Mark my words. One of these days, you'll be measuring your net worth in bullets, not cash." She wondered if he was also a woman playing this drag-reversal game. Not possible, she concluded. She had seen him pissing on a scotch pine. That kind of aim required the old hoser.

"Yeah? What kind of bullets?" she asked. She instantly regretted her smartass remark. He didn't seem like the kind who would go for the Beatrice-Benedick "merry war" kind of love-sparring.

On the other hand, she could see LOVE/HATE written all over Private Luddy's face. He had joined for probably all the wrong reasons—a grudge against all authority figures, a need to feel important, a place to chunk grenades and an audience to listen to his lies about having gone skydiving from 15,000 ft.

Tonight was ALL POINTS RECON night. This was going to be a difficult night for Traynor and she was looking forward to the challenge. She had lied about her military experience (she had none) and she had no idea what the weird acronyms and buzzwords meant. It was exciting. She wondered what would happen if she just strung together the first nuclear-submarine-movie-spy-novel-Cold-War-hysteria words that popped into her head.

She figured the best way to seduce one of these camouflage-&-ammo guys was to pull off one of those fraudulent & campy "I'm the leader" bullshit trips. She would ape a television documentary interpretation of Patton. Of course it would come across as a weirdly skewed tough guy. Her voice was not a male voice. Her legs were slender. Her hands were delicate. Her fingers were thin like piano wire stretching around their necks. Her eyes were star-blue guillotines. If only they could see her breasts under her fatigues.

"Let's get a lock on those coordinates so we can take in the collateral positions before they call in the infra-red to get numbers, profiles, density," said Traynor. Her heart pounded at the audacity of it all. She felt sweat bead up under her left breast.

"We've got to maintain the PAC."

The 40 or so militia members seated in folding chairs under the galvanized roof of this old converted dairy barn nodded in agreement.

God knows what a PAC was. She made it up. But, it seemed to signify something. Her success made her brazen.

"The SPRINT lines are fibered so that they listen in. We've got to get our own COM lines nailed down or it's burst 90 rounds per minute on our asses," she continued.

They laughed at that. She had no idea why.

So far, no one seemed particularly taken with her. Seducing these guys was going to be an uphill battle. If only she could wear her Santa's Little Concubine teddy and thigh-high white fishnet stockings.

"Too bad you're stuck with the dummy rounds," mumbled someone in the group.

She was trying to go for the geekster-expert role. Someone wasn't buying it. Of that she was sure.

"I know for a fact that they're listening in. They want to know what we're up to. Scan lines in the night vision glasses. That's from interference."

"Hey. What makes you so sure?" said someone in the group. Was it Private Luddy? She couldn't tell.

"I've seen this configuration a thousand times, and each time it makes my nuts sweat." Traynor had always wanted to say that. She shifted her weight slightly like she had seen guys do when they got twisted up in their shorts but didn't want to make a spectacle of themselves while untwisting.

"Yeah, they're monitoring us, that's for sure. We can't pick up anything. We're being jammed," said Walt, who claimed to be a former intelligence officer. He was sitting next to Luddy. She could sense that they'd buddy up together—make it one of those male bonding rituals. They'd say it was about "doing the right thing" but it was really about how they were scared as hell to say anything on their own. Plus, they knew in their heart of hearts that they didn't have the capacity to stick with anything.

Losers, thought Traynor. Easy. Maybe too easy.

"They're trying to get a lock on our positions again tonight," said Traynor. "We've got to keep moving. If they're doing infra-red, we've got to scatter. Quick."

A few of the men in the group looked at her oddly. She wondered if she had bungled by not using enough acronyms or incongruous euphemisms. She thought she'd better try again.

"Remote sensing—they've got the resolution to nail us down to the pixel—false color composite," she improvised from LANDSAT data.

Before she had a chance, Mark, a guy she had already categorized as a paranoid whiner, took the bait. What a freak, thought Traynor. The guy would be so much better off doing what his type did in the outside world—he'd make a great women's shelter manager or liquor store night manager.

"I think we've got another Area 54 on our hands—obviously they've got equipment impounded in there," said Mark. He was sweating and his hands were pale with excitement. "I think they're going to start bombarding the captured UFOs with radiation, electromagnetic vibrations and ultra-high frequency transmissions. Does everyone have their shields in their packs?"

Traynor relaxed. This was going to be easy—where was Private Luddy?

"That jamming may not be jamming," said Traynor. She let her voice sound paranoid. "They're out for us—I think they mean business. We're a nuisance to them—a dangerous nuisance, and well, Mark, you've got to be right. They're bombarding us with toxic rays. They don't want us to make contact with the extraterrestrials—no, that would be way too risky."

"Can anyone draw up the coordinates tonight? Luddy?" she asked.

Walt and Luddy were gone. Good. Plotting mutiny, she said to herself.

But, who died and made her Queen of the Militia? She was a newcomer. They were indulging her tonight because she was hitting all their pleasure points—conspiracy theories, UFO's, secret abduction and training sites, black helicopters, secret monitoring.

The group stayed up all night discussing the government's conspiracies to hide the fact that, ever since Hiroshima and Nagasaki, the earth had been visited by extraterrestrial ships and creatures who were drawn to Earth by the great big welcome mats of mushroom clouds and radioactive jetstream.

"You say that Truman was thoroughly briefed when the first extraterrestrials were sighted?" Traynor wondered what it had been like in the War Room during those long, hot nights after the bomb.

"Of course. You knew that, didn't you?" LeRoy looked up at Traynor. She hoped she had bound up her breasts enough. Her baggy army surplus fatigues should hide anything, she thought.

"No. I was in the military, remember? We were fed disinformation. I wasn't in one of the missile silos that were visited on a regular basis by the extraterrestrials," improvised Traynor.

Traynor wondered how the militia members managed to take a perfectly good & titillating topic—GOVT ATTACK & COVERUP OF UFOS—and render it utterly lifeless. She wished she had stuck with reading the *Weekly World News* headlines and forgotten about this quest to show her obnoxious cousin Robert that militias were the last bastions of wimpy-ass patriarchy, where all the members longed for the good-old-days when a land-owning white guy was truly King of the Tobacco Road and all the rest of the unfortunate rabble were stuck doing the old why-should-I-work-at-love-when-I've-got-you-to-bone-in-the-woodshed number with dear old paternalist dad or his fat, sweaty, dissipated sons.

What she wouldn't give for a little woodshed action now, thought Traynor.

The militia members were a confounding lot. Their aggression made them provocative, but Traynor was beginning to suspect that their paranoia grew in direct proportion to their inability to function in the bedroom.

Is Eden still Eden when there's an AK-47 in every apple tree? What happened to the nice, taut, sinewy snake?

This was it. This was what she was surrounded by—limp, hysterical, paunchy, dogmatic, speech-making bores. How disappointing. Not one pistol-whipping, no mock trials, or threats of execution. No loyalty tests. No hazing. No urinating on the new guy (or woman). No forced oral sodomy. No naming of the Antichrist. No laser tattoos on the butt. No macrobiotic diets—just salty and tasteless MREs and a strong stomach for self-righteous posturing. What a bore.

After the meeting adjourned, it was Traynor's turn to stay in the militia's own equivalent of the War Room. She logged on to Internet to see what e-mail messages had come in from other militia hotheads around the country. There were 12. The subject lines were pathetically transparent—RE: MANEUVERS, RE: OPERATIONS TONIGHT, RE: YR AREA.

"After listening to you, Traynor, we've decided you're full of shit," said Luddy. Traynor jumped. She didn't realize someone had come into the War Room. Walt was with him. They looked drunk.

Mildly bored, she began reading the messages. They all had the same long-winded paranoid interminable droning tone except one: "WHY DON'T YOU STOP PLAYING SOLDIER BOY & GO BACK HOME?" It was from someone with the screen name "GUESSAGN."

She clicked on "Reply" and typed, "Your message sounds enticing. I'm sorry I can't write you a lengthy response. I'm in the middle of torturing a hostage. But, maybe I can take a break for you."

"Hey. Listen to me when I'm talking," said Walt. Luddy stood next to him playing backup.

"I'm busy. I'm on guard duty for Paradise," said Traynor.

"You're on duty for something else," said Walt. Luddy had a glazed, drunken grin on his face. "According to Nietzsche..."

"According to God, Nietzsche is dead," returned Traynor. "Because we killed him."

"Why don't you just go before we ask you to leave?" said Walt.

"What do you want anyway?" said Traynor.

"We want you to shut up and listen," said Luddy.

"Okay," said Traynor. She threw off her battle jacket and started unzipping her pants. "I'll shut up. You've got to do just one thing, though."

"What's that?"

She was naked.

"Fuck me."

Afterwards, she wondered who had really won her little game.

Royal Family

"You ran away!" A quiet-looking man in a white Nissan Sentra is shouting and whispering into Ronald McDonald's mouth. The McDonald's drive-thru is crowded at this time of day, and he has just placed his order. In the passenger's seat is a stack of biographies of Diana, Princess of Wales.

"You want fries with that?" The staticky voice sounds bored.

"You weren't supposed to let us down." Plastered onto the book jackets, Princess Diana is unruffled by his obvious anger—her smile does not waver.

In his eyes, however, everything wavers. He imagines Ronald's mouth twisting into a taunt. The lips are mouthing something to him: "You'll never have her you'll never have her you'll never have..."

"Please drive through."

The drive-thru, with all its emphasis on patience, queuing, and orderly payment of the expenses of one's own hunger, reminds him of the theater, the spectacle, the madness of a court wedding. Disappointment always follows fast on the heels of resplendent display. This is what he refuses to accept.

"Yes?" The woman's voice startles him. Someone has stuck a bumper sticker on the menu:

> Your rearview mirror tells you more
> about tomorrow than what is behind you.
> Objects are closer than they appear.

He looks in his own rearview mirror but it unfolds nothing but the past, with footage of Lady Di's wedding. Diana is coming down the steps from the cathedral in her vast, white, virgin-princess fantasy dress. She is smiling, teasing, taunting. He is chasing her, but she doesn't see him. He whispers, "You promised—"He hears a rush of music—impressionistic music of Debussy mixed with the strains of Abba.

Horns are honking behind him. He drives forward, digs through the change in his ashtray and hands it to the woman at Window Two. He recognizes her assistant as Princess Diana, but by this point he is not even surprised.

"It's been an empty shell of a marriage for a long time now." Diana is standing near the drive-thru window, lifting the fries basket out of the deep fryer. She's talking to the drive-thru cashier. She has worn her tiara to work.

"I want to start getting on with my life." How does she do her vowels like that? Like thett? She's scooping a super-size fries box into the fries.

Shame is the flip-side of faith. Lost faith equals shame. Losing faith in kings, queens, empires, crowns, and Ronald McDonald. What next?

He felt, like the rest of the world, betrayed by Diana—betrayed by a monarch who just wouldn't shut up and preserve the illusion that if you're born or become rich and powerful, you'll be happy.

"Here's your change, sir." Diana is holding up a pocket mirror and applying bright red lipstick. She starts with her lips and works outward, creating a clown mouth. Will it be a sad clown or a happy clown? He doesn't stay around to find out.

★ ★ ★

The closest he ever got to Princess Diana was at London's Gatwick Airport. He was just back from an overnight trip to Paris and was sharing a dried-out croissant and sipping thick, warmish coffee with an American woman he thought he could dazzle with his European charm.

He liked her because she was blonde, dressed like an American, and talked with a Texas drawl. He could teach her a thing or two about culture, he told himself.

"My name's Dorene McHenry," she told him when they first met.

"Ay, a Scottish lass," he said, trying to be cute with a brogue.

"Cut it out. I hate it when people try to be Scotty to me. That Star Trek shit makes me puke."

"My name's Philip Sidney. No one calls me Phil."

"Okay, Philip," said Dorene.

"You're not going to ask me if I'm descended..." he began.

"Oh, you mean if you're Sir Philip Sidney of Renaissance England—wasn't he gay? I didn't think he had any children," she said.

"Hey—just because I have a Texas accent doesn't mean I'm illiterate."

"So now I've taken you to see the Eiffel Tower, the Arc de Triomphe, the Rive Gauche—that was Paris by Night, my dear."

"I didn't expect Paris to be so smoggy and expensive."

"Now don't worry yourself with that—this is my Welcome to Europe present to you."

"Oh, yeah. Thanks for going with me. You're too generous. I'm tired," said Dorene. She was a regular Hollywood Singing Cowboy in her bolo tie, western jacket, and cowboy boots. Give me cactus juice and a red-hot branding iron. I could get to like this big-sky life, he thought. Nature is inherently cruel.

Someone had programmed the television next to gate announcements and flight information to the new YESTERDAY'S NEWS channel. The Windsor Castle is on fire. The Queen Mother is shuddering in pain. After the hip replacement, she could no longer claim that her constant pain was simply physical. It is raining, but moisture only seems to make the fire angrier and hotter. The windows are streaked with tears, the firemen's rubber coats drip with grief. There is wet soot on the Queen Mother's pink wool coat. She is the most beloved of the Royal Family. She wipes soot from her chin with a soot-stained handkerchief. It only makes the stain worse, but she doesn't know that.

Philip fingered the sterling silver Windsor Castle charm on his keychain. He had always thought of grandeur as an antidote to pain—existential pain. With grandeur, salvation was possible. It made it possible to look at the monarchy and imagine a benevolent and generous God. He could imagine the heaven from which we came, the heaven of our reward. God did not have to be an inner responsibility.

Philip's Jaguar wouldn't start at first.

"British engineering," he laughed. "We could have never made it to the moon—that's why UFOs come to us. They know we could never come to them."

Dorene laughed. "I've never seen a UFO. Have you?"

"Yes. They're fast and they go places. Faster than you can imagine to any place you can imagine."

"No way," said Dorene. "You act like they come whenever you want, whenever you ask for them."

"You have to believe. That's the first step."

"What's wrong?" she asked.

"This isn't a good place to be stranded like this. You're going to have to help, my little chickadee. Start praying for an alien abduction in your cute little Texas drawl if I can't get us started."

"I'll pray for the aliens with guns in their pockets who are happy to see me."

He opened up the bonnet and adjusted the starter wires. It was taking more time than he had hoped. Dorene sat in the car—pale face, dark circles—a far cry from the florid, self-satisfied, smug and stupid look he attributed to Americans. By her expression, she looked torn as if by some internal civil war. What did she have to be haggard about? Since the Cold War, the U.S. was strong, dangerous, and armed to the teeth. It could dominate the world with its standing army and bloodlust driven by its staggering debt.

"There. All ready to go," announced Philip.

"I'm tired. I haven't slept in 72 hours."

Jet-lag was slipping a bag over her head. He had seen it before— it would asphyxiate her, then it would slip off gradually, in great tearing gasps. He knew he could get away with anything while her mind was made subordinate to the body's craving for sleep.

"Don't worry. I'll get you home and tuck you in straight-away."

He followed the signs. WAY OUT. TOLL BOOTH. Was the English spoken here inherently politer, more indirect, more deferential than elsewhere? Was class consciousness instilled by means of the language of one's own thoughts? He often called himself "sir" in his own daydreams.

Dorene had fallen asleep. She seemed not peaceful at all.

He pulled a ten-pound note from his wallet to give to the parking lot attendant. To his surprise, it was Princess Diana. She was wearing a tiara and working the cash register. "5 pounds, please."

"Excuse me, but you look remarkably like—"

"Yes, I've started working two jobs now. I think everyone should have a contingency plan."

"Why? Isn't that what the dole is for? Time to retrain? Shouldn't you be spending time with your boys?"

"I want to be an inspiration to my sons, and I wouldn't want them to expect their future wives to be superwomen. That is the curse of the last half of this century. Besides, it's ethically incorrect. If I spend more time with them, I'm stealing a job away from at least three hardworking, deserving women—one cook, two nannies."

"To be a parking lot attendant?"

"No. To be a free-lance worker in life—a researcher of society and its mores—an anthropologist on Venus—a scientist in the laboratory experiment of self, identity, and changing roles."

"You mean you're showing us that you're giving up. Times are tough for everyone. You're bankrupt, and you won't admit it. Why didn't you have insurance for Windsor Castle? You just let it burn. History burned, heritage burned, a people burned, and you didn't care. It wasn't like wartime. Bombs didn't cause this. Philip was smoking in bed with his lover. The Royal Family burned its own castle and its own traditions. What do you have to say about that?"

"What's your name?"

"Philip Sidney."

"Philip Sidney. You didn't leave off the 'Sir' I presume." Diana sighed, handed him his change. "Oh God—you, too? Another one. Has the whole country gone bats? I suppose you won't ever admit your real name."

Dorene stirred in the seat beside him.

"Who're you talking to?" Her cactus flower earrings jangled as she spoke. "I don't see anyone."

"Welcome home. We're back in Londontown now, my little Yankee friend."

"Now you sound like the Ghost of Christmas Past. Don't you have a real voice, Phil? Who and what are you anyway?"

"My company has exclusive license to market and distribute postcards and pictures of The Queen's Dollhouse," said Philip.

"What's that? The best little whorehouse in Hampstead Heath?" asked Dorene.

"No. I'm sorry, that honor goes to The Keats House. The way

they've made that a sordid tourist attraction..."

"I guess I didn't want to know anyway. I don't really understand you, Philip. We've known each other for 24 hours now—ever since you met me for lunch, then said you'd go with me to Paris. Usually on a road trip, you get to be pretty good friends with someone, or you at least get to know what makes them tick. I have no idea about you."

"The Queen's Dollhouse is just that. An elaborate replica of Buckingham Palace. In miniature. We do quite a good business—but we must always give something back. Immigrants forget that."

"Are you talking about recent arrivals from the old commonwealth nations? From India? Pakistan? Jamaica?"

"Yes. Of course I am," said Philip.

"Don't you think they gave enough? I mean, England basically stripped them of their resources and their labor—and artifacts," said Dorene. She yawned. "I'm so tired I could collapse right here. Can you take me to the Hampstead Inn? I've got reservations."

"The Hampstead Inn? That's a good choice. They sell quite a few Queen's Dollhouse postcards in their giftshop. A young woman named Shari runs the shop—she has quite an appreciation for the monarchy."

"Now Phil, if you ever come to Texas, we'll give monarchy a run for its money. You may have your London Tower and your Madame Tussaud's Waxworks and Jack the Ripper, but we've got the Alamo, Pace picante sauce, and armadillo chili that'll wipe that smile right off your face."

They pulled up to the Hampstead Inn. A thin white man in ragged riding pants ran up to the car. Philip recognized him immediately. It was Prince Charles. "Your windscreen need cleaning?" He held up a dirty rag and a squirt bottle of bluish-green liquid.

"Good heavens, have you no shame? No! Now leave before anyone sees you! Why are you doing this?" asked Philip.

"Everyone needs a contingency plan. That's what I always say," said Prince Charles, in offended, clipped tones.

"Why were you so mean to that man? He wasn't going to hurt you," said Dorene. "These bags are heavy and I'm exhausted. Too bad he didn't carry the bags instead of clean your windshield."

Philip carried her bags to the entrance of Hampstead Inn. He stood awkwardly as he fingered his Windsor Castle key ring. Prince

Charles was running up to a rusty Volvo that had just pulled into the drive.

"Thanks, Phil. That was great—if you're ever in Texas, look me up."

"Right, yes, thank you." Philip kept staring at the pathetic wreck. He noticed a urine stain on Prince Charles' pants, and a rip in his left boot. The man stared at Philip. Philip averted his eyes.

"I can't figure you out, Phil. But, that's okay. I don't have to know or understand everything—it was fun in Paris and thanks." Dorene entered the hotel.

Philip returned to his Jaguar which now had oil streaks on it from Prince Charles' divine absolutions.

"Haven't you any shame?"

"I need the money, man," shouted the skinny man, who was busy smearing up the rusty Volvo.

★   ★   ★

It was a cold, foggy morning in Paris, Texas—foggy in the way London used to be when coal fired the houses and the factories. Philip had driven to this town directly from Dallas, after a non-stop flight on British Airways from London's Gatwick Airport.

He looked down at the postcard he had taken out of his Daily Reminder book. On the front was a picture of a freshly painted Victorian house.

GREETINGS FROM PARIS, TEXAS

The card was addressed to him. The message was brief, but cheery.

> *Hi Phil!*
> *Remember Paris? Don't let your life*
> *become a bad Sam Shepherd play!*
> *luv ya,*
> *Dorene*
> *p.s. call me sometime!*
> *(802) 326-1242*

It was postmarked December 28, 1995, Paris, Texas. Was this what she meant when she said to visit him? It had been almost two years, but he hadn't been able to get her out of his mind. After their trip to Paris, he had started to see other members of the Royal Family in various demeaning or dirty jobs around London, and even in the suburbs.

He wished they would stop. It was bad for business. No one seemed interested in the Queen's Dollhouse if it was no longer a symbol of monarchy—the closest possible visible link to a higher order, a realm of perfection.

He pulled into the parking lot of the Best Western Paris Inn and entered the hotel office.

"Can I help you?"

"I'd like to ring up a friend, then check in. Is that all right? It's a local call." said Philip.

On television, Princess Diana was attending a 12-Step Program for Bulimia, Anorexia, and other Eating Disorders. "I just always thought my body was very ugly and that I could never be thin enough or pretty enough. You see, I always considered myself defective."

The monarchy was between humankind and divinity on the Great Chain of Being. What was happening?

Charles was on a talk show. "I was in denial until I realized that what I had was a compulsive need to have sex. There is a clinical term for it—simply put, it is sex addiction. Once I realized my powerlessness over sex, could begin to change. I am powerless." He was seated on a small throne-like chair on stage. The caption reads, Charles, Prince of Wales, Prince Regent. The prince looks as though he will break into tears.

"Dorene?" A woman's voice answered the phone. "I got your postcard—I'm calling from Paris. Yes. Paris. Paris, Texas."

The volume on the television began to increase. Princess Diana is on again: "I see the failure in our marriage as a problem of self-esteem. We had a storybook marriage, but even fantasy cannot compensate for a profound rejection of self. It is, I've come to see, an existential condition—the only way I had to express that, though was through binging and purging. Now I regret it. I thank my Higher Power..."

"Dorene! I can hardly hear you—I'm shouting? Sorry. This television. It must be jet-lag, too. I'm going to go for a bit of breakfast. Will you meet me this evening? For a drink? I'd like to see the Alamo."

The man at the desk turned to Philip. "Is everything all right?"

"Chipper-ho," replied Philip in a David Niven voice straight out of a late night movie channel.

Philip noticed a McDonald's down the street.

"I think I'll get breakfast. See you soon."

He smiled at the desk clerk, but pointedly ignored Prince Charles, who was digging through an ashcan, looking for old cigarettes.

The Last Bait

In Madill, Oklahoma, the myth of the eternal return comes in flickering neon and burned-out language that should advertise rest, but only gives tired eyes a glimpse of a half-drunk fisherman in a dirty cowboy hat pouring dead bait into a gutter and a fat young woman spraying mosquito repellent onto her ham arms:

TH RETURN MOT

The owner's wife once spent most of one long evening arguing that they should rename the motel, "Le Bon Mot." Just what is that "bon mot?" asked the husband. "Shit," she said.

After that, he didn't even bother to fix up the old sign. That will teach her, he said to himself. After a few minutes—after the time for a snappy comeback had long passed—he thought of a witty rejoinder. It was too late. She had disappeared. He heard water running from the taps full blast in the decrepit motel bathroom she had turned into darkroom. When she emerged, her face was red and puffy. Years ago, he might have wondered if she had been crying. Now he just stared at her. She hadn't been crying. She had an eating disorder. Therese was bulimic.

Therese and Buck had a relationship that had started out as a shared vision—now they both would say delusion—but it had ended up as shared blindness.

And she was very sick—sicker than anyone might imagine—but she wasn't telling. And Buck couldn't begin to guess.

"You okay?" he asked, as he had asked many times before. Therese stared out the window with glassy, bloodshot eyes. Her voice was hoarse.

"What difference does it make to you?" Her nose was running. She jerked the back of her hand across face.

"Screw you, too." Buck slammed down his beer.

Her barely-suppressed rage made her pervert her abilities in her dismal, claustrophobic darkroom. She became a master at the dodge—printing two negatives over each other. Therese believed it was her calling to conjoin disparate images—to be-strange nature and perception.

"What you think is 'normal' is completely abnormal!" she shouted to him over coffee one morning. They were standing in the motel office and were watching a man put up a sign on the back of his camper:

Day-Glo Dave's Nite-Crawlers.

To illustrate her point, she dodged into the night—her favorites were combinations of Lake Texoma nature shots and what she called "Creature & Miracle Art" culled from the neighborhood used book store.

On those long nights, her darkroom gave off an evil stench of developing chemicals. It masked the smell of vomit. She wrote in her logbook: My view of the world is alien and strange—but it's my reality—it should be other people's but they won't open their eyes! Her throat was raw and tight. Sometimes she was afraid to go out of the darkroom or the motel, even during the day.

She could hear Buck snoring from the bedroom behind the office.

"Why are you doing this, Therese? Why not spend your time fixing up the rooms? Or, why not make flyers for us to give out at the tournaments or to put in the Tourism Department's HOWDY, YOU'RE IN OKLAHOMA NOW! Welcome Centers."

"Who gives a shit about this shithole," snarled Therese. "These pictures will make us money."

"How?" asked Buck. "What is it?"

"It's fucking reality, *mon petit chou-chou*—"

"Reality?"

Therese snickered. "Look at this! Real? Fake? Doesn't matter?"

Buck looked at the prints she had strewn on the table. SCENES FROM TEXOMA BASS TOURNAMENT was etched on each one. They looked real enough until you looked closely. On one, was a man's head coming out of a trophy fish held up by a proud man wearing waders and a cowboy hat. "Not real? Doesn't matter?" asked Buck, bewildered.

"Wrong answer! Wrong wrong wrong wrong—always wrong!" said Therese. "Open your eyes!"

Outside in the parking lot, Dayglo Dave was gluing fake bait to his back window. The plastic nightcrawlers were lurid and slippery-looking.

"If you want funny shots, why not just take a picture of him?" asked Buck.

"Fuck you. You don't get it." Therese got her camera and took a few shots of Dayglo Dave and his camper. "I'm just doing this to make a point."

Buck finished his coffee, put down his mug. "We need more coffee. You want to go to the store with me? I'm going to check into having a postcard stand at the Bass Tournament office, too—maybe we could sell your THE ONE THAT GOT AWAY postcards there."

Therese's thin face crumpled like linen in the pale morning light. "Buck, I love you—you know that don't you—you're too nice sometimes and I don't know what it is—Buck—" Suddenly she was crying.

"Therese—what's the matter? Should I stay?" asked Buck.

"No, no, no—just go ahead—I'll be here," said Therese. Buck kissed her on the lips gently, wiped her tears.

After he had left, Therese stormed out the door and walked up to Dayglo Dave, who was still gluing plastic nightcrawlers to his left camper window. "Are you Dayglo Dave?" she asked.

"Yeah. Wanna buy nightcrawlers? I'm running a Bass Tournament Special here. Two for a dollar, a dozen for five bucks."

"No. I want you to leave our parking lot. Get your truck and your maggots out of here. We do not sell worms. We are a resort motel and you are bad for our image."

"This fleabag dump? A resort motel? Lady, I'm GOOD for business. And I can be good for your business, too, hon."

"Keep your nightcrawler in your pants, you maggot," said Therese.

"Suck my dick, you foreigner. Go back to your own country." He spat a wad of Kodiak chewing tobacco onto the pavement.

"You go back to your dirty hut with your sister!" she shouted as he peeled out of TH RETURN MOT   parking lot.

★ ★ ★

Her desktop contained her latest dodged prints, which she had labeled. They included: Bigfoot coming out of a camper trailer; Bigfoot caught bass fishing; A white, glowing cross and a disc-shaped UFO hovering over a moonlit lake; Pickup trucks with stained glass windows; The head of the Madonna caught in an old Big Mac wrapper litter.

Therese was a good Catholic.

She began to develop the roll of black and white Ilford film that contained the shots of Dayglo Dave and his plastic bait. While the negatives were drying she looked at what she might dodge them with. In her mind was the same old debate—why not cut and paste? Why not photomontage? Why not collage?

Dodging is imprecise, ragged and you don't have so much control, mumbled Therese. Just like life.

She started the process. A closeup of a nightcrawler lure got combined with a shot of Oklahoma sky. There were worms curling around the edges of the clouds. A shot of Dayglo Dave looking back at TH RETURN MOT   got combined with shots of giant fossil nautilus shells on the shores of Lake Texoma. Dayglo Dave was turned to stone, like Lot's daughters fleeing Sodom. His camper was combined with an old tabloid photograph of extraterrestrial beings, so it looked like Day-glo Dave's Nite-Crawlers truck was the secret headquarters for a new War of the Worlds. A closeup of Dayglo Dave was combined with a shot of a fish hatchery so that it looked like fish were coming out of Dave's mouth and the nightcrawlers were there to harvest them. Therese etched a caption onto the bottom of the print:

> In the end, those who were BAIT
> will become FISH,
> and FISH will become BAIT.
> The EATEN will EAT,
> the EATERS will be EATEN.

It was late, and Buck was still out. She imaged he was at a local bar—perhaps the Paradise Club on U.S. Highway 70—drinking a few beers, sharing fishing stories. While the prints were drying, she got out the half-gallon of Rocky Road ice cream and the pack of Vienna Fingers she had purchased earlier from the local Piggly-Wiggly grocery store. In a trance, she opened the lid and started devouring the entire contents—methodically with digging, stabbing motions of the spoon. After every five or six bites of ice cream, she ate a Vienna Finger. She polished off the half-gallon of ice cream and pack of Vienna Fingers with three cans of vienna sausages. Vienna! she thought. If Beethoven had died of a ruptured stomach, would anyone question why? The veins in her neck and belly throbbing, she went into the bathroom, leaned over the toilet, and began to purge. Halfway through, it occurred to her that Buck might return. She got up, dizzy and hot, and turned on the taps. The sound of running water didn't really mask anything, but she didn't know it. After she had finished, she lay down on a folding cot and collapsed into a deep and distressed sleep. Her face was puffy and the dark circles under her eyes were too deeply etched to be relieved by sleep.

★ ★ ★

The day was clear and cold. Therese shivered. The Bass Tournament was dragging on. In spite of Therese's rudeness and the motel's dinginess, a few of the rooms were booked. Across the street, at Hobo Joe's, the parking lot teamed with campers and pickups emblazoned with rod, reel, gun, tackle box, and bullet decals. Someone mounted a big deer rack to the inside of a camper shell, and multi-colored bobbers were hanging from it like Christmas tree ornaments.

Therese once drew a picture of a woman biting an enormous hook attached to the rod and reel of God. In the picture, God was hairy and he looked a little bit sad. He had already caught one fish—it had *agape* branded onto the scales. That fish was a woman, too, filled with roe. Therese drew the picture so that one wondered whether or not God would spare his catch of Love and throw it back into the lake—mutilated but alive—or whether it would be fried up to be served on a bed of rice.

She hung the picture in the motel office under the Coors waterfall clock and over the Scenic Oklahoma calendar.

"Take that thing down. They'll burn me alive, Terri," he said.

"Damnit, don't call me Terri. You know I hate that." She looked at her drawing and snickered as she prepared to take her nightly Valium. It was the only way she could endure living with him.

Life wasn't so great with her either, thought Buck, her husband. He comforted himself with the fact that he knew they were both still intensely and deeply attached to each other. Why ask why? he often said to himself. A lot of people would envy me, he continued.

They had met years ago while he was on a fishing trip in northern Quebec, where she was taking photographs for the *Destination: Les Vacances* (Destination: Vacation) issue of the Sunday supplement of the leading Montreal newspaper.

One night, as he was showing her how to fry brook trout over an open fire, and he told her about his dream to open a resort hotel on the Oklahoma side of Lake Texoma.

Years later, they still hadn't made it out of this fisherman-on-a-shoestring-not-quite-nirvana flophouse, Terri & Buck's very own Eternal Return Motel. Her pride kept her from admitting to anyone back in Montreal how bad this really was.

His pride kept him from admitting how rude she really was to him—how she seemed to make it a sport to humiliate him. You hooked me, Therese—you've reeled me in—isn't that enough? he often thought to himself. But then she'd kiss him, beg him to make love to her, and would shower him with affection all night. He'd wake up happy, but confused.

Life with her was no picnic. Picnic? Hell, she'd probably puke up a picnic, thought Buck. He knew Therese seemed to suffer from chronic nausea she sometimes attributed to food poisoning, sometimes an incipient ulcer. He didn't realize that Therese had a long-standing eating disorder. It had come on gradually—about the time they had remodeled the motel office and bought new TVs for the rooms instead of making a down-payment on a charming, flower-garden bed-and-breakfast that was for sale on the posher, high-dollar Texas side of the lake.

I'm a stupid fool, he sometimes told himself. What on earth was wrong with her? He had first thought that perhaps she was pregnant, and her complaints about nausea and her frequent trips to the bathroom after eating were symptoms of morning sickness.

But soon it was clear it was much too strange for morning sickness—and too long-lasting. Six, eight, ten months rolled by—no

"First Alert" pregnancy tests, but a lot of weird cravings. Spam & ice cream. Peanut butter on pumpkin pie. Peanut butter and sardines. Godiva chocolates and Cheez-Whiz.

"Therese?" Buck decided that the pickup truck that had pulled up to the office might stop and not just use the parking lot for a U-turn.

"Therese—where are you?" he called out again. She needed to clean up the dirty rooms. This could be a good weekend. But, they'd have to get the room presentable if they expected to have people in there, he told himself. "Terri?"

"Don't call me Terri!" the sound of her voice echoed against bare walls. She was in her makeshift darkroom. The smell of photographic chemicals was nose-burning and acrid. "Hey, why don't you do that at night! It stinks. It drives away customers!"

Therese slammed the washroom/darkroom door behind her. "What customers?"

★ ★ ★

The next year's tournament was bigger and better than ever. The organizers took in more revenue than ever, and the businesses that served the fishermen were booming.

"Ma'am, do you have a room for the night? I know it's the Bass Tournament and all, but my wife's pregnant, and she needs someplace to rest tonight." A sunburned man with a Texas accent and an open Schlitz beer can walked up to the front desk.

"If she's pregnant, why is she fishing in the Bass Tournament? Are you sure she's not just a little flabby in the belly?" asked Therese. She sounded almost Cajun, she was drawling with irony. The man glared at her.

"Hey. We're good repeat customers here. We stayed at your place last year, and now we're back. You should be grateful," he said.

"Where's your wife?" asked Therese.

"She's out changing a flat. We must've run over a nail or something," he said.

"And now you've returned," said Therese. She thought of the driftwood washed up onto the shores of Lake Texoma during the annual rainy season. That was also tornado season. The violence always comes back, thought Therese. It's the most predictable of all.

"Do you need any new lures? We just got in a fresh supply for the tournament." Therese pulled out a fishing tackle box and plopped it on the registration desk. She opened it up—in it was a full selection of relatively hideous and very garish worms and other blobby shapes.

"Gawl-dang. I ain't never seen nuthin' like thems," said the man, exaggerating a backwoods accent for effect. "Do they work? How effective are they?"

"They are simply the best," said Therese, exaggerating her Quebecois accent in response. "They were first developed by fishermen in the North Country. Would you like to see photographs?"

Therese pulled out a portfolio of photographs and showed him a print of a man fishing from a boat, with a tackle box of her worms in the boat. The water was clear—in the region around the line and the bobber, you could see the shadowy presence of enormous fish. The legend read, "Lake Champlain." The next photograph featured a fisherman holding up an enormous striped bass. Next to him, was what appeared to be a window with worms glued onto the surface. The word NITE-CRAWLERS was barely legible.

"Man alive. I'll take some. How much are they?" he asked.

"They're two for a dollar, a dozen for five bucks. They really work," said Therese.

The man's wife came into the office. "Whoa, am I tired," she said. She picked up a card from the counter.

> Eternal Return—
> Bait that has them coming back
> again and again!

The logo was an ourobouros—a snake swallowing its tail.

"Hey hon, let's try these out," she said. Her husband picked up his Schlitz and took a swig.

"All right. We'll take ten dozen," he said. "You won't be sorry," said Therese. "By the way, we might have one room—it's small and hasn't been remodeled. If you want it, I can fix it up."

★ ★ ★

"Well, I've finished cleaning up Room 14," said Buck. He was carrying a mop and bucket. "The bathroom floor was covered with some sort of goo. It came up easy enough, but it sure looked strange."

"Oh I forgot to tell you that's where I cooled off the first batch of lures. The gummi worms turned liquid after I microwaved them on HIGH," said Therese. It had been six months since she had last binged and purged.

"How'd you ever get the idea of microwaving gummi worms and jellybeans?" asked Buck.

"Hell, they taste good when you eat them together—sweet an not-so-sweet mixed together," said Therese. "And they look good dodged together—microwaved, I mean—together."

"Yeah, and we can eat what we don't sell," said Buck, laughing.

That night, Therese microwaved together a batch of gummi worms and jelly beans—these were in loops—nightcrawlers sucking on their own tails. She put Christmas tree hooks on them and hung them up under a sign that read:

STOCKING STUFFERS
DO YOUR CHRISTMAS SHOPPING
EARLY THIS YEAR.

The management of Hobo Joe's bought 5 dozen for their Christmas tree. For a star, they put a carved striped bass with agape painted on the side. Hungover one morning, Dayglo Dave stopped in for bacon and eggs one morning, saw it, and started shouting at the waitress. The manager threw him out.

Wildcatter

I'm writing from a cabin in northern Maine. I hope no one finds me. I'm not quite sure where I am, anyway.

I don't want anyone to know I'm here.

What happened? At least there are no oil and gas wells in Maine, and nothing to disrupt the natural flow of family ties. I was there when the whole thing came crashing in on itself.

And now I don't want anyone to find me.

It can be hell working for a family business.

My uncle spent years on an impossible quest—he was convinced there was a giant oil field still hidden south of Slaughterville, Oklahoma, in township 8 north—range 2 west.

My father spent years trying to create a utopia. I like to think it was after my mother died, but who knows. Maybe it started before that. I don't even remember her. I was 7 when she died, but I hadn't seen her for years before that—she had been stuck away at some state mental hospital and no one even dreamed of "stabilizing" them with medication so they could be "transitioned" back into society. Besides, she had tried to drown her child—me, that is—in the downstairs claw-footed bathtub.

But, mother is mother. I felt a great deal of loyalty toward my mother—a woman I imagined was misunderstood. She was probably the long-lost progeny of the long-lost Anastasia, princess of Romanov Russia. That was my favorite daydream. Of course, I knew it was a daydream. But I liked it. It had a nice ring to it. Plus, it would explain why I always thought I was somehow different from others— not better, just different.

When my dad turned 65, his quest for utopia became more urgent. And more embarrassing. He took up with a woman who called herself Razpah who first caught my eye with her sense of fashion. It was pure gypsy in the most unimaginative and Halloween-costumed way possible.

I rather liked the pure, unadulterated camp of it all. She reminded me of a female impersonator I had once seen at a performance art festival in Tulsa. "Justine" was a "bondage gypsy" with lots of piercings, leather collars, wrist cuffs, and over-the-knee boots. There was a sign draped over the stage when she performed: Good conduct well-chastised! Then she sang her theme song: "I'm Very Very Good, So Spank Me!" Everyone laughed, whether or not they recognized the allusion to the Marquis de Sade.

I could imagine Razpah as a dowager-bondage gypsy, a fascinating older-woman version of Justine. I could just picture her with just a few more scarves, strands of beads, and silk ribbons, singing "Tie Me Up Before I Get Too Loose" or "Only 30 Lashes? Can't I Please Have More?"

But, it was impossible to maintain these fantasies. It was especially difficult when Dad was so intrigued by her. He insisted upon foisting her upon me as some sort of surrogate mom.

"Do you like Razpah? She's quite an interesting woman, you know," said Dad one day after a long evening in the field. We were sitting at the conference room in the office and looking over the Midcontinent mineral ownership maps for the counties we had just studied.

"I guess she's okay."

"She has been helping me a lot," said Dad.

"Helping?"

"Yes. She's a great help," said Dad.

"Well, I don't care what you do, Dad. You're a big guy. Just don't let her into the business—she doesn't know anything about finding oil," I said.

My deepest fears were coming true. She was "helping" Dad develop oil and gas prospects.

"I think you need to keep her completely away from the office, Dad. She's just after your money," I said.

Of course Dad ignored me. The next thing I knew, Razpah had supplanted me as head geologist.

My uncle was affected too, but he was too busy trying to show me up to see it. He didn't even realize it meant we were out the door when Dad announced Razpah had developed a new geophysical technique that could detect undiscovered oil and gas reservoirs from up to 500 miles away.

"Have you ever seen her work?" I asked. "She's not a geologist. She's a map dowser! She doesn't know anything."

"Why don't you give her a chance? What makes you think she's not a bona fide explorationist?" asked Dad.

"Well, Dad, it's like this. One night, late at the office, I noticed the light in the conference room was still on. I went in, and there was Razpah, hunched over a map. She was holding a crystal attached to a silver cord and asking questions in a deep, guttural voice."

I went on to tell him that she was a fraud in other ways as well. Instead of her usual Hungarian accent, she had an accent I identified as pure Texarkana. I slipped off before Razpah noticed me and before I got a chance to witness the whole routine. I know what it was though—some called it "map dowsing." It was like the "witching stick" without the stick.

"I wouldn't be too skeptical if I were you," said Dad. "There's more to map dowsing than meets the eyes. Have you ever read about quantum mechanics, space, time, and fractal geometry?"

"No," I said.

"Razpah's technique is a part of the 'new science,' and unless you've really read Schrodinger and Einstein and Fermi, you won't understand," said Dad.

"Do you have to read about a con artist to understand what they do?" I muttered under my breath.

Dad was completely mesmerized by Razpah. I would not have cared, except that it was screwing with the business. Plus, she had the nerve to pander to my uncle. She told him his Slaughterville prospect would be a giant oil field—more than 10 million barrels. Of course, that won him over instantly. She pronounced all my prospects worthless. After that, I started calling her Rasputin.

"Her method really works," said Dad. "Oh, yeah?" I asked, "what has the old fake come up with now?"

"She understands wildcatting. In fact, I think Razpah is a true wildcatter. You're not. You're too conservative," said Dad. "Yes. She's a wildcatter. Just like me."

"She's a hag," I said. "Not a wildcatter."

Wildcatter: 1) A person who engages in high-risk oil and gas exploration efforts by drilling in places far distant from established production in hopes of finding significant new reserves. 2) An adrenaline junkie. A compulsive gambler. A dreamer. A visionary. A glutton for self-destruction.

The victims of Rasputin end up in shallow graves. The victims of Rasputin think they're something special. They think the stars will protect them. The victims of Rasputin will lose their identity. Everyone wants to be Anastasia.

Now I'm in Maine. This is not Oklahoma. Oklahoma is one continuous ghost-town of dreams and polychromatic mirages slicked like film on the surface of a puddle of once-potable water. I keep trying to forget, but my thoughts intrude.

Maine is the refuge of those who know it's pointless to fight. It's the place where the defeated go to deny defeat. Besides, as far as I know, it's my ancestral home. It contains the shallow grave of Justin Wilcox (1714-49), the first of my dad's family to come to this country. By all reports, he was a very decent, good man. Too good, it seems. According to his diary, which my grandfather gave to the Maine Historical Society in exchange for a tax break, Justin suffered from "dark dayes" when he became "mindefull of the spirituall afflicktions importted by the Englishe to America." He hanged himself the day after Easter in 1749.

My grandfather built a small log cabin on an overlook, near the old family cemetery that contains Justin's grave, as well as the other ancestors who didn't have the sense to get the hell away from land contaminated with suicide vibes.

I can stay here in the cabin, at least until the dead cold of winter sets in. It's free. And, it allows me a chance to buy time until I can decide what to do next in my life.

And, at least I'm still alive. But, I'm the only one who knows that. Rasputin has most certainly interpreted my absence as the fulfillment of her prophecy that I am cursed by my mother's demons and that I have probably killed myself.

They had a way of discounting my observations when what I said didn't reinforce their big plans.

"You're obsessing about finding oil, and Rasputin's just playing your obsessions," I said.

"How many times do I have to tell you not to call her Rasputin? Her name is Razpah!" said Dad, miffed.

"What you don't understand is that Rasputin understands all about obsession," I told my father and my uncle. "And, unfortunately, you don't."

They ignored me. Of course. My uncle's obsession was also his way of saying he wasn't ready to see things the way they are. He saw a giant oil field just a few miles south and east of his house. Good? Maybe. Problem was, it was covered by a town. And a quicksand & water moccasin-infested river. Just how did he plan to drill for in the middle of that? Put up a barge? Stretch his hide across the nearest sand bar & prop the rig up against his ass?

"Obviously, you're just jealous," said my uncle.

My uncle and Rasputin would have made a cute couple—in hell. Or in Waco, Texas. They could have double-dated with David Koresh and Lois Roden, the 80-year-old lover of Koresh and founder of the Branch Davidians.

Rasputin and my uncle both played upon Dad's utopian delusions. They both did it just for the sport of it. It wasn't as though they really needed the money or the glory. They just liked to see people fall under their spell.

They weren't going to get me. I'm no wildcatter. I'll never be. I hate wildcatting. Wildcatting is for cowards who can't face reality. Cross my palm with silver, my ass. To think that one has been placed under a curse is an extension of one's grandiosity. I'm not a part of any kind of cosmic dialectic between good and evil. I just want to smack the shit out of Rasputin. Claw her eyes out. Take the silver out of her palms and spend it on cheap beer and cigarettes.

But, what power did I have? Rasputin said, "DRILL!" and we did.

Then came Razpah's attempts to befriend me.

"Cross my palm with silver and I'll burn a candle for you and protect you from your mother's curses."

"What makes you think I'm cursed? And, what makes you think my mother was cursed, or that she cursed me?" I asked. I was shocked.

"Sometime in her past, she did very bad thing which made her hear the voice of the devil. The voice of the devil will now come to you if you don't do something to get rid of the curse," she said.

She actually seemed serious about what she was saying.

"What do you know about my mother?" I asked.

"Many, many things your father has told me. She died alone," said Razpah.

"You think that if a person suffers from schizophrenia or depression, it's because they've done something bad, and God is punishing them?" I asked.

"No. God has cursed them. And their children," she replied.

"Where have you been? Under a rock?" I asked. "It's been pretty well established that mental illness is a chemical condition, and it's sometimes genetic. Besides, who decides what 'crazy' is?"

"Then why are there so many exorcisms?" asked Razpah.

"I don't know. Is this a riddle? Okay. Let me see. Because an exorcism holds out the promise of an instant cure? Because an exorcism can separate you and your identity from that of the 'demon-possessed' one? Because fear and intolerance are easier than adjusting to another person's idiosyncrasies? Because there are a lot of people who would like to be 'instant priests' and conduct exorcisms without actually taking the training and vows of a real priest?"

"I'm worrying about you," she said. "You don't know the curse. It is strong. Powerful. You have nightmares and you don't even know it. You think your dreams are ordinary dreams, 'cause that's all you've ever had. But these dreams are demon-dreams. They will make you want to kill yourself," said Razpah.

"Why is that?"

"It puts the Death-Mark on you and if you don't kill yourself, some-one else will do it for you," said Razpah.

"And you're going to tell me that's what my mother did. You don't even know the story. You only know what my dad told you—that my mother tried to drown me because God told her that the Devil made her pregnant, and that I am really the daughter of the devil," I said to her.

"You need to believe me. It is for your own protection," said Razpah, in a loud, hoarse whisper.

"My mother didn't try to drown me. She thought she could wash my blouse without taking it off me. She was rinsing it!" I was really upset that Dad would tell her these very intimate things.

It was the weekend of the Rose Rock Festival, named for twinned barite crystals found in the red soil near town. My uncle was con-vinced that this was the best possible time to build the location and spud in.

"But there are going to be parades & cow-chip throwing contests during the Rose Rock Festival," I said.

"They're not going to be throwing cowchips around our drilling operations," my uncle said. He looked at me coyly. "Razpah says that Jupiter and Mercury are in Aquarius."

"Stuck in the '60s, huh? Did she ask you to cross her hand with silver?" I asked. My uncle assumed a miffed expression. "Why're you so touchy?" he asked.

"Because I'm sick of cannibals and bullshit and bloat and squeal-like-a-pig experiences in my own back yard!" I responded. He looked a little taken aback.

I guess that was no excuse for what happened later. I have to justify myself somehow, I guess. Now I'm in northern Maine, in a two-story cabin that looks nice enough on the outside, but doesn't have electricity, phone, or other contact with the outside world.

My father's old, trusted friends tried to wake up my father to the realities of the situation. "You're being taken for a ride," they said. "Razpah's method doesn't work and neither does yours, for that matter. Why don't you retire?"

Of course, that just irritated him and made him all the more determined to prove them wrong.

Remorse isn't much fun. Craftwork in the middle of uncharted territory. I'd rather promote a made-in-the-hinterland product than hitch up with a truckload of reckless quilts, accompanied by foolish women who say the key to their success is a flexible smile and relentless ceremony. It really couldn't be much worse. I've sold all my possessions. I'm traveling light. I'm experiencing a lightness I didn't know existed. Lightness. Lightness of the problematic.

In a local gift shop, The Rose Rock Gallery, I saw a single rose suspended from the ceiling. It was a multi-petaled sermon-in-stone someone decided to appropriate for a festival. Rose Rock. Interpenetrating crystals. Lives that engage in each other's structures in spite of themselves.

Why not just settle for the simple life? Crystals don't have to twin, psyches don't have to fragment.

Sure.

It's dark now. I hate the whine of mosquitoes. I like the sound of water on rocks. Naragansett Stream flows into the Connecticut River near here. Would anyone guess I'd come here? I'm not sure I care any more. I'm gambling that no one will find me.

My uncle might wonder. My father should not have tried so hard to do the impossible. I'm in the mood to blame someone. Could that be me?

"How does Rasputin's method work, anyway?" I asked. "Her name is Razpah. Why do you mock her? What's your problem? What did she ever do to you?"

"The question is, what did she do to YOU? You're under her spell," I said.

"What do you have against her?" they asked.

"She's ruthless. She'll off anyone who gets in her way, but no one will ever know she has offed them. They'll think she did the world a favor. She'll have them committed or stripped down so they can't do anything at all," I said. They looked at me oddly. My uncle put a wad of Red Man in his lower lip. It was time to go out to the well.

Our biggest investors, Heinrich Schliemann and his wife, were sitting in the back seat of my uncle's white BMW. Heinrich's wife had confused a junkyard for an installation of *objets trouvées*.

We had just approached the quarter section of land I call Maytag Ranch, after Cadillac Ranch just west of Amarillo. The old Maytags were lined up under a section line of Dutch Elm-diseased trees, not arranged according to model but according to fractally significant clusters of Harvest Gold and Avocado Green.

A guy in overalls and a plaid shirt was approaching us.

"Can I help you?"

"Sir, have you been reading Georges Bataille?" I asked.

He looked at me and dug a wad of Red Man chewing tobacco out of a pouch and stuck in his cheek.

"Yes'm. I sure have," he said.

"What do you do with all these?"

"I adjust their frequencies." He sat on the top of an avocado green one.

"What do you mean?" I asked.

"Each one has its own frequency of vibration. You sit on it & it will stimulate your own vibrations." His accent became more southern as he got more Reichian.

Investors were driving up to the location. My uncle, was trying to convince himself of his geological authority. My dad, was presenting the best case possibility: "If we hit oil, if we offset, if we develop the field..." Me, I was making sure I didn't wear my purple leather driving gloves, my Raybans, my big fake-fur coat, Dalmatian-print boots. I wore jeans.

A billboard stretches out overhead:

> Frontiers of Oklahoma:
> Invest in the NEW Technology

I was tired of investors dragging their dreams into my reality. Investors making a play for "mind-share"—that is, I had to start caring about their interests more than mine. Did they know that these prospects were all based on Rasputin's whims and butt-twitches— her "intuition"?

Sure, we showed them the "traditional subsurface geology"—but all that was negated by Rasputin's map dowsing.

Maintain concentration, I reminded herself. It would be easier if I could wear a better disguise than anonymity.

Investors didn't want the small reservoirs—they didn't want to hear about 50 mcf per day of natural gas from a coalbed methane seam. They wanted 500 barrels a day from the first of many wells drilled in a field. My father wanted to prove that the old eternal verities were lies. Death isn't death. Not everyone "dies"—everything is just as you perceive it. You can train time and space to obey you. Death won't be so scary.

Frustration.

The nights are already cold in northern Maine, even though it is still August. Rain in the afternoon, shrouds of fog in the morning. Fish embellish the ambiance by jumping.

I'm hoping no one will figure out I've come here. If they know me, they'll think of coming here. It's obvious. My father's family owned this land for 8 generations. It's nothing to be proud of—it only keeps me rooted in the past—in my genetically-determined capacity for mayhem and self-destruction.

Right.

The skies and the trees are just too unmanageable when they come in contact with the American myth of the eternal frontier. Streets paved with symbolism, and all that. A white dove. A red hawk. An ant carrying six times its weight in food.

Rasputin lumbering along with bowling balls for an ass. What would they say if they knew such a quest would rob him of his mind and condemn his children to the ledges of hell he himself should have visited?

She asked all the right questions: "Do you believe in a soul? Have you ever noticed that things don't make sense? Do you think your dreams are more real than real life? Do you know how powerful you can be if you train your mind?"

Rasputin probably would have gotten to me, too, if she had been a man and had not worn those embarrassing disco-gypsy togs.

I hated that we always drilled dry holes and that all our ventures were failures. But it didn't make me want to put my "faith" in Rasputin. There was more to it than that, I guess—there was my "ethical and existential dilemma" (as I used to refer to it.) The man selling ice cream during January made his living hustling a concept. Preservation. Too bad it was only in the form of endless sleep, or a mound of ice and a frozen popsicle stick. Sleep was a wrapper of dreams to keep the thaw away. My arms felt wooden when I had to describe the latest prospect.

I never got used to it. Each time we plugged a well, I had a migraine attack.

"If your head hurts, take an aspirin!" My uncle was a master of the cliché.

Don't stick an ice pick up your nostrils to cure a transitory pain. The predictable pain was like walking barefoot in the snow around a well about to be plugged and abandoned. After awhile, my toes were numb. Frostbite didn't hurt.

"Can we drill a well to test the coal seam? It's low risk. We know it's there, and that it will produce. The question is how much."

"Why should we mess around with coalbed methane?" he asked. "Because it's low risk," I said. "It's not high-risk when you've got a method that tells you where the oil is," he said.

I was being unfair, I suppose. Now I see I only have the capacity to justify. I've broken with my beliefs and now they're coming out like miniature trains through long, dark, unilluminable tunnels.

Perhaps Rasputin is right. Perhaps I have been affected by the past, by history.

My mother is speaking to me from the dark of night: "Wash your blouse. Rinse it. It has the smell of skin. Skin is what stretches over you and keeps you from bleeding. Skin is the lie. Rinse out the smell of the lie that suggests that you don't bleed your soul out onto the street each and every day. You and I are the same. We both lose everything and no one ever knows how much it hurts."

From where I sit in this split-log cabin, I can see that analogies break down into their component parts. Figurative speech lets me find sympathy for myself in an inanimate object. Not that it matters anyway.

Inappropriate, undeserved guilt stands in my way. I would prefer to be arrested if it could mean I could come face-to-face with various devils. Rasputin is only a convenient excuse. I can blame everything on her. I don't have to talk about fear.

I wanted to create a place for myself in the midst of the risk and hopeless dreaming. However, there isn't much I can see from here. Was it necessary to go the way I did? I disappeared. I did it in a way to cause maximum disruption. Was that so wrong? Yes. Probably.

It's just so hard to be angry all the time.

Years before Rasputin, we drilled about five wells a year. For the most part, they were successful. Yet the returns were always uncertain. The uncertainty could get to anyone—that's what made one vulnerable to a Rasputin.

"I don't want to become a grifter or a used car salesman," I told my uncle. "Huh?" he replied. "What are you talking about?"

I decided to confront my uncle about Rasputin. We were at La Brujería, a local Mexican restaurant. My uncle was flipping pennies into the wishing well fountain next to us.

"Down on your luck?" I asked.

"Yeah, sure," he was silent for a moment.

Without humility, life treats skin like razors run over sandpaper. Ceremonies always seem to end the moment they begin. Is that what you might define as predictable? Map dowsing mimics ceremony, but it's only narcissism, like all rituals that claim to give one secret knowledge.

"Rasputin's going to ruin us," I said.

"Her name is Razpah. What's wrong with you? Why don't you give her a chance?"

"Have you ever asked her where she's from? What did she say? The Carpathian Mountains? I think she's from the swamps of Texarkana."

"Razpah likes my prospects and she recognizes yours are shit. That's the only thing that is 'wrong' with her." My uncle ordered a specialty drink, "El sacerdote."

Outside the sky was working reds against the blues. Wheat was just turning yellow. Who could ever conceive of a happy, bright labyrinth? I remembered swimming in a pool and hearing meadowlarks. Scissortail flycatchers were perched on telephone lines. The sky was filled with invisible labyrinths. Minotaurs must have been in the clouds, not in the dear yellow light.

Sunset was trapped in my uncle's eyes. The beaks of reason were turned inside-out in an attempt to explain surrender.

The next afternoon I became convinced my dreams had begun to go into someone else's body.

I dreamed I was in a department store when a car bomb went off.

Doctors were extracting long slivers of glass from my abdomen and my eyes. I felt sharp ripping as they pulled against my gut. But then I saw my dreams slip into another person's body. Did the recipient of my dreams feel that pain? Was I responsible?

I did not will my nightmares away. They simply slipped out and did their damage in a random, uncontrollable way.

I kept dreaming of big, ugly machines that represented work, not freedom. My dreams could not even free me since they since they themselves were comprised of semiotic equivalents of work & thus they chained my mind to the concept of work even as my body craved to be free.

Is this what it means to get older, to lose your dreams?

The next night, when I dreamed, it was of children hunched together in a circle, flailing a cat with lotus blossoms. Buddha said all sweat comes first from the mind, only second from the energy field you persist in calling your body. So, who feels the pain? We all do. We are connected.

"Razpah works with energy from the stars. If you read Schrodinger, you'd understand it," said my father.

"If you read Reich, you'd throw her away and use your energies in a better way," I said.

"I don't understand what's gotten into you lately. Have you thought about seeing someone?" he asked.

"You mean, like, go out on date?" I asked. "Or, are you saying I need to see a psychiatrist?"

"Just talk to someone. Deal with some of this hostility," said Dad.

"Get rid of Rasputin," I said.

"That's what I mean," he said. "Razpah likes you. She says you're like a daughter to her."

"Oh my god, I'm going to be sick. You fell for that?? This is not about filial anxiety, this is about money. Reality. Dollars. Oil. Maps," I said.

"I can make an appointment for you, if you'd like," said my father.

"NO!" I said.

The rain starts early here, then goes away sometime in September. The fall is sometimes warmer than late summer. It's hard to explain. Maine is filled with ghosts. But still, I'm glad I'm here. I hope no one finds me.

Memories. My sunglasses were sliding down. It was hot and sticky in the field. We were near Slaughterville, and we were looking for a place to build a road into the drilling location. It was routine, but sunny. The sunlight broke in my eyes and reduced my vision to blind abandon. Some called it hallucination. Rasputin called wildcatting a philosophy.

On they way to the location, I saw a train fall from the sky. Metaphors posited a false connection between my moods and the rings around Saturn. Saturn's rings are not wedding rings, but its satellites could be considered analogous to anniversaries. Some are cold and frozen. Others are covered by active volcanoes.

"Why don't we ever drill my prospects any more?" I knew why. My low-risk prospects didn't excite my uncle or my dad—or the investors, for that matter. "Razpah has looked at your prospects, and they're not any good. Sorry."

I'm here in Maine. I'm fighting memones.

I'll awaken and I'll wonder if it dropped into the 30s. It is cold. Painfully cold. Cold hurts more when you realize you're existentially alone. We all have places we need to avoid. Mine happens to be something I can't talk about yet.

One summer, I took a cure in Switzerland, and the spa was only an hour from Lugano. Flowers filled my thoughts as if memory could wash my consciousness. Velvet wrinkles. I tell myself that if I have been good, I will become more caring and alive as the years pass. I didn't want to hear about the downside of it all. Sure, we had some success. But it seemed to bore my uncle and my dad. They didn't want to develop the fields they found. They wanted to keep going, keep moving forward. The old American promise of endless frontier (to the white boys) had been translated into another language. "Go West" became "Go Underground." Seek the depths. They are illimitable.

It took a machine to enter that garden. I named that rig Chronos. My first choice was "Chiron," after the deity who ferried souls across the River Styx. The drill rig wasted no time taking us into that prelapsarian garden of layer upon layer of dank, compressed earth, which sometimes yielded the exoskeletons of species extinct for 60 million years.

After Rasputin took charge, we always tested the formations at night.

Dream-sounds-pup-pup-pup-my lips pursed around the knowledge of what I had just seen in the samples the drill bit ground up. It was usually disappointing. Breakfast was warm coffee and a roll smashed into the wall. *Ma poupée*—my doll—in the midst of remnants of war, ruined walls.

Here I am now in Maine, and I'm trying to forget. The walls fall in on me, and grass is burned by the pressure of loss.

I understood very little of the mirage that rose up in front of me in the field near Slaughterville. I was just looking for a place to build a cheap, gravel road.

I would rather lose myself in the loneliness of a uniform, than in the uncertainty of this "independent" life. The voyage was something I took with my eyes, and not my heart. And still I realized how the refusal to believe in another person's delusion is a final good-bye—to the mother, the father, even to the grillwork of the elevator and the concessions to Newtonian physics that keep you safe. To protect myself, I separated my mind from experience. All seemed to promise eternal innocence, eternal dedication, and devotion.

The promise was the form of narrative I hated most. It was the mirror-twin of the prospectus.

My coat had a pocket large enough for a small, paperback metafiction called *Build Your Own Road*. I never bothered to take it out.

The gnawing inside is not hunger, but I feed it anyway, every day. When I woke up one morning, I had that familiar, terrible shaking, nervous, panic-dread feeling. Hunger. Feeding. Loneliness. Running away. Not running away.

"She can detect more than oil and gas, you know," said my father. "Razpah can detect paper money and coins. In fact, she told me that some of our neighbors have been carrying large sums of cash in the trunks of their cars."

"You believe that?" I asked.

"She can detect people and their frequencies. She told me she's worried about you. Your frequency has been undergoing a disturbance. She considers you a daughter, you know," he said.

"If you think she's so wonderful, why don't you do her a favor and take her shopping for clothes. K-Mart would be an improvement. Rasputin in clothes manufactured by child labor. That would be appropriate."

"Her name is Razpah."

I gave up. I decided to take my mind of Rasputin and take a drive. I drove to Boley, a small farming community located on the border between the Sac & Fox Nation and the Creek Nation. Jim Thorpe was a member of the Sac & Fox Nation, although his mother was Pottawatomie, and buried in the churchyard at the Sacred Heart Mission. I found her grave accidentally one afternoon. It was cool, quiet, and sad. The grass needed mowing. I wonder if she knew that her son would be a hero. Jim Thorpe's twin uncle died when they were nine years old. After he died, Jim began running away from the school he had been sent to. They made them go to Indian boarding schools in those days. No one ever says why, except for the great intangibles, such as "assimilation" and "a future."

The last prospect of mine we had drilled had been a partial success. If it weren't for blowout preventers, we would have lost the well. The crew was nice to me. They acted quite chivalrous—they carried the bucket full of samples to the trailer for me, and offered to catch samples at 5-ft intervals instead of 10-ft. "Thanks but no thanks," I said. I was shirking my duty, some might say. They didn't understand. I would look at 5-ft samples, but only near the zones where I expected oil and gas. It was just too much work, and it delayed things too much to catch too many samples too early in the day.

I looked at the sky and I saw it sweat. I was surrounded by people and noise and gorgeous, lush Oklahoma bottomland, but still I felt disconnected from humanity.

It is dark outside. A single pinpoint of light is shining from within the forest somewhere across the valley in Vermont. Here in Maine, I think it is completely dark.

Survival belongs in some antiquarian gift shop. It's too expensive to buy, so it is necessary to find contentment in the simple observation and appreciation of it. Look but don't touch.

"I have an announcement to make," said my father. We were drilling ahead. Rasputin couldn't stay away. My father was planning the next well.

We were drinking coffee at the Slaughterville Git 'n' Go. Next door was a quilt shop. Crafts represented the miracle of forgetfulness, wrapped up in a blanket, wrinkled with hope.

Dad had pulled out his pocket calculator and was doing figuring out return-on-investment. It was all pointless, because a good ROI presupposed a discovery of oil and gas. I didn't expect any oil at all to usher out from Rasputin's filthy maw.

"Razpah and I have a little announcement to make," said my father. I felt my arms grow cold.

"The Bolsheviks are coming?" I made my voice as sardonic as possible, considering I was about to weep.

My father ignored me. Rasputin took a sip of coffee and smiled evilly at me. "I consider you like the same as a daughter," she said, in her thick high-camp fake-gypsy accent

"Razpah and I have been talking about the future," said my father. "We're going to make some changes."

"And where's the honeymoon gonna be? To where they found Anastasia's bones? To the old ancestral palace," I paused. "In Texarkana?"

"Razpah has detected a supergiant gold deposit in South Dakota, and buried treasure in Iowa. We are going to explore for it together," said my father.

"What about Slaughterville?" I asked.

Rasputin cut me off. "Look at your daughter. She needs professional help. She's so sad. She can't think, she can't eat right, she can't even say what's in her heart—listen to how she's all mixed around. The frequency is in big troubles. She's like my very own daughter and I want to help or have her helped. She needs to be with doctors in a hospital, maybe," said Rasputin.

"Nothing is wrong with me!!" Of course they didn't listen to me at all. "Don't lock me up!"

Maine is cold in late August I hate the cold, but I prefer it to the alternatives. I hope no one finds me. They don't need to know, and I don't feel like explaining anything. But, then I want them to find me. I want them to know why I preferred to run away, and let them think I had committed suicide. Maybe I will. I don't know. Something seems to be pushing me to pain and self-destruction. Are these the "dark dayes?" Am I Justin or "Justine"? Will I be punished for depression or for "good conduct"? Either way, the people in my immediate environment seem to think I don't fit in. They seem to expect me to do something horrible. Why and how can I stop it?

Shadows of pine and spruce on the wall. Dreams take the evening chill into the space beyond reality. I should call my aunt and ask her how to crochet, how to knit. I could construct a covering for myself which is more lasting than any disguise, any mask. And maybe it would even keep me warm. There's no phone out here.

Let me go.

Let me go.

Let me go.

My consciousness will not let me go.

The whine of mosquitoes outside the window screens makes sadness all the more real. Unlocking the box containing matches, lighter fluid, and keys to the Jeep requires an act of memory, an open beckoning of nostalgia. I'm still walking barefoot through chilled forests where time has become lodged in the wet moss and dripping blueberries of promise. Mortality manifests itself as intertextuality or polyphony. I drape my rinsed-out washcloths and towels on a clothesline. They will sleep, even if I cannot. The weather is as disturbed as a bird hatching itself, pecking out of the shell.

They think I killed myself. But I didn't. I simply ran away. That seemed better than having to confront them with my true feelings—that I was going to need to admit I didn't believe in wildcatting any more.

What does it mean now, to be gone from Oklahoma, gone from that life? I'm here. For now. I could have left a note, but I prefer for them to draw their own conclusions. They never listened, so what difference did it make? I fantasized about telling everyone—investors, uncle, father—"This is not good for me—I get nothing out of this but the feeling of fraudulence and shame. I've got to get out!"

But I couldn't.

I listened to the people at the table next to us. Slaughterville had a wide variety of people, despite the first impression of white bread and pasty asses.

A woman was talking next to us. "Yesterday, in anatomy lab, we dissected a cadaver of a woman who was in her 30s, but her organs were like a 60-year-old. Her pancreas was a total ulcer." I was in no mood to listen to anything. Rasputin's hold on my father (and my uncle) was slippery and vague. The woman just wouldn't shut up. "They said this woman was in bad shape for years—she wouldn't make the changes she needed to make. So her pancreas ruptured. Sick, huh." My stomach hurt. My head throbbed. Rasputin handed me a scrap of paper with writing on it. Coffee, coffee, coffee, my body screamed. "Can I take your order?" I couldn't answer.

Outside, Slaughterville fell apart in my mind's eye as bright light on water droplets, or turbulence within the depths of a clear, glass bowl.

My uncle used to drown ants in the root beer he made in the cellar of the cabin I'm in right now. Ants. Humanity. They drown as a result of their own insatiability.

Yesterday, I pulled weeds from around Justin Wilcox's grave. The marble headstone is barely legible.

Tomorrow I'll find a clear, glass bowl, fill it with fruits and vegetables from the woods and from the garden, and then I'll place it next to a blender, a mixer, and an industrial bread machine.

Yesterday, I mailed an order to an Italian monument company with a check for a headstone carved with my mother's name.

Tomorrow, they'll find me.

When my uncle, Rasputin, and my father ask me why I ran away, I'll just tell them it was a twentieth-century thing. Madness, I'll say. That won't make much sense, of course, but that's why everyone will believe it and go on. In the meantime, I'll just go on finding meaning in nothing and nothing in meaning. In the meantime, there's something else. They refuse to understand. I refuse to try to change them any more.

Yesterday, I mailed a check to the Italian monument company. I sent it with a detailed description of a small headstone to be elaborately carved with vines, trees, and angels. There won't be a date, but there will be a name: "Justine."

Tomorrow, (or on some tomorrow after that) it will arrive. In the meantime, I'll just go on finding meaning in nothing and nothing in meaning.

Maybe I'll order a dozen or more headstones, all inscribed with the name, "Justine," and I'll lay them out like Maytags in the cold, Maine dirt.

And that's what I call "wildcatting."

Tia Erqueminia: Diviner of Destinies

Tia Erqueminia, "Diviner of Destinies," opened and closed her eyes in what I thought was a gesture entirely too theatrical for her own good. I looked at her with not much more than vague indifference.

I had decided to kill time in her storefront office next to La Confitería El Rosal (Rose Tree Pastries), one of my favorite places, drink a cappuccino and watch the traffic snarl up on the Avenida Mariscal Lopez, the main thoroughfare of Paraguay's capital city, Asunción. Ordinarily, I rather enjoyed watching as impatient drivers trapped pedestrians in the mayor's latest brainstorm, the little cages in between lanes he called "pelícanos" which were supposed to give pedestrians a place to rest as they crossed the street. Of course they were death traps—cars and buses regularly plowed into the rest areas, crushing the pedestrians who couldn't leap out in time.

Three months ago, back in the U.S., I had finished a long study of the use of propaganda in World War II and the early Cold War, and I had developed a severe case of paranoia. My family suggested a long vacation, so I decided to move to Paraguay for a few months. This was, of course, an incredibly illogical choice for a person suffering from paranoia, given the country's history of human rights abuses— the bloated corpses of "los desaparecidos" showing up in the Paraguay River, their hands wired behind their backs, their jaws exhibiting empty tooth sockets, their extremities displaying badly healed fractures.

But that was in the past. Paraguay was now experiencing democracy—which meant more freedom, and, as a side benefit, more violent crime, bank failures, corruption, and unemployment. I decided to stay for a few months.

The "few months" had slid past, and a few months more. It was time to go, but I had fallen in love and I wasn't in any great hurry. The only problems were these long, dull stretches of time.

La Confetería El Rosal was closed for remodeling (they said, although I didn't see any activity inside) and spending some time with Tia (Aunt) Erqueminia sounded better than getting back into rush-hour traffic. Her flyer promised to "tell me the story of my future."

"Do you have time to see me?" I asked.

"Do you have $25, US currency?" she asked.

"As a matter of fact, yes," I said.

Now, the "adviser over spiritual subjects" was asking me a few questions as she looked at the cards I had selected:

"Have you ever travelled to Africa?"

"Are your parents divorced?"

"Were you ever a model?"

The fact I answered NO to everything didn't discourage her a bit. Her voice was hypnotic. She kept going:

"Did you recently sell a white Mercedes?"

"Is there a pregnant woman in your office?"

"Do you like things made of glass?"

My answers were the same: "No, no, and no." I was beginning to think my investment of 25 dollars for an hour of "advice" was going down the drain. I was already feeling a little bored.

My mind wandered. I imagined myself talking to Fidel Castro on his secret ranch in the Chaco about a few of his more arcane tastes: his Paraguayan Moulin Rouge cabaret acts featuring Guarani Indians all wearing white stockings and smoking Honduran cigars.

"How can you abuse them that way?" I exclaimed to Fidel Castro. "Honduran cigars?"

"Of course not!" responded Fidel in a brusque voice. "I'm sick of these Yankee idiocies! How many times will we have to endure these atrocities! They are Cuban cigars. I would never buy imperialist products!"

"Please forgive me, Sr. Castro."

The sound of Tia Erqueminia's fingers shuffling the cards caught my attention. She kept asking questions.

"You're thinking of getting married, eh? Did you know there's another woman?" she asked me.

"What?" My spiritual "counsellor" succeeded in getting me to pay attention. I looked at Tia Erqueminia, really for the first time, with a mixture of caution and curiosity. There wasn't anything remarkable in her appearance; she was a typical South American with blonde hair, glasses, medium height, and a face that exhibited what one might have said was sincerity, if she hadn't selected the scoffed-at profession of psychic, provider of New Age services.

"Yes." To me, her voice sounded satisfied to have hooked me. Her game bothered me a little, but she had won. I wanted details.

"It makes me sad to tell you this, but it's better that you know now rather than later, right?"

"No. I would prefer not to know."

"The other is a brunette, with long hair, medium height, and is a little chubby."

"Chubby?"

"Fat. And when you're not in Asunción, your boyfriend visits her. They've had this relationship for years—she's divorced and is crazy about him."

"What? You're kidding! I don't think I really want to know any more." I felt a little desperate. Her "revelations" were beginning to give me a stomach ache. I had never been a jealous woman, but one could always acquire unhealthy habits.

To tell the truth, it depressed me a little to think that the person who had promised me his eternal devotion was betraying me this way. When I reflected upon our history, yes, I could detect a few small indications that there might be problems in paradise. It was true—he was something of a control freak, and he expressed dismay that I refused to wear long fingernails or keep my opinions to myself.

Did being a scholar of propaganda make me its biggest victim? My problem was that any patently manipulative and coercive discourse fascinated me. I had to see it through, regardless of the consequences.

Tia Erqueminia was speaking.

"I see things—maaaaaaany things," she said.

"Like what?" I said unenthusiastically. What bad luck I always have with my life, I thought. Evidently, it gave me great pleasure to persistently choose the bad. It was disheartening to see myself such a masochist. It was probably hopeless.

"What can you tell me about my future?" I asked the "advisor."

"Your fiancé loves you very much, from the time he first set eyes on you, he totally lost his head," she said.

"Really?" I felt a little better. That was only temporary. But, if he wants me so much, why does he keep going out with another woman? I suddenly felt very surly, and in a very bad mood. It was just as well that I had 20 minutes left. Maybe Tia Erqueminia could help me. I gave her a rather aggressive look. She glanced back at me, startled.

"Your fiancé is going to give you a beautiful engagement ring. An enormous diamond," she said.

"Seriously? That sounds good."

"Yes. But it is going to be false."

"How horrible!"

"Your fiancé is going to ask your father to lend him $100,000."

"What? Who? A loan from whom? My father? But my father's dead."

"Minor detail. Your fiancé, when you're married, won't let you leave the house."

"Por favor! That's too much. I can't believe it. How's he supposed to keep me locked up inside?" It's the old "mad woman in the attic" routine, I thought. Well. Little did she know that it rather appealed to me to wear rags and scare the shit out of people who messed with me.

"I don't believe in this. I only came here to kill time."

"The cards never lie. I know it can be hard to accept."

"What if I DON'T accept it?"

"You have to. It's what is in the future and it's the truth you've kept under a veil," she said. "Yes. There's another woman."

"Oh."

A series of revenge fantasies entered my mind. One I would borrow from Pedro Almovodar—I was in my kitchen, preparing cream of ham soup, when I grabbed the hambone destined for the soup and began to smack everyone in the room. First, I clubbed the psychic with the bone, and next the swine I had had the bad luck to fall in love with. Smack! Too bad it wasn't very likely to come true. Too bad I'd end up in a Paraguayan prison. Better to save it for a propaganda film, I thought.

"Do you have any questions?" Tia Erqueminia asked me.

"No. I'm afraid to ask questions," I responded.

"Okay. That will be 25 dollars."

"Do you accept credit cards?"

"No. I only accept cash. Either pay me or I curse you."

Curse me? Let me curse you! Oh well. You've already cursed me with your vile predictions, I thought, but I didn't say it. I only hoped the psychic wasn't psychic enough to hear my thoughts. Evil bitch. Fake diamonds? Kiss my ass.

"Well, thank you very much. Have a nice day." I gave her her 25 bucks and took off. I almost tripped over a cluster of quartz crystals she had put in the dirt near the entrance. She put it there to leave her mark—bruises—on the pathetically naive suckers who fell into her scamming hands. I looked at my own hands. They were trembling, and covered with sweat.

★ ★ ★

Once again, the sickening subject of "love" had reared its squalid head. Tia Erqueminia only confirmed what I already knew.

It was best expressed by the old Gang of Four album I used to listen to daily: "Love is like anthrax and that's one thing I don't wanna catch. I'm like a beetle on its back. Love is like anthrax..."

Actually, for me, love was less about disease and/or plague and more about stupid choices. But, denial is a hard thing to shake. So is the tendency to be charmed by men one could only call decent if one were in an extremely generous mood. I generally fell for all of them. The weirder the better. There was the "Executive Director of the International Pigeon and Dove Institute," for example. "We're going to build a huge theme park and museum, and call it 'World of Wings,'" he informed me within two seconds of meeting of me.

"How are you going to get the pigeons there?" I asked. "Put out a bunch of park benches?"

"No," he replied coldly. "We are going to race pigeons."

"Oh," I said. "Raise pigeons?"

All I could think of were a million park benches covered with dung, and mobbed dumpsters, like the one behind Dunkin' Donuts next to the McDonald's where I went every morning to drink very hot coffee, munch on a breakfast burrito and read the morning paper. Over the years, the Dunkin Donuts dumpster become a well-established nesting area. I suppose that would be called a "loft."

"Yes. That's why we are locating ourselves next to Remington Park," he replied. He made little birdlike jerks with his head.

"Where they have horse-racing?" I asked incredulously.

"Absolutely. We plan to have pari-mutuel betting with the pigeons, too."

I was left speechless. Here was an entire facet of life that I had previously not had any idea existed. How fascinating. You could bet on pigeons? So how did that work, anyway? You take them out into the country, far from their homes, and then dump them off, so they have to do a *Lassie Come Home* trip, all the while feeling lost, panicky, and far from home? That sounded cruel to me. If homing pigeons crave home so much they'll kill themselves to get there, isn't it wrong to take them away from their homes?

"Are you going to have cock-fighting and pit bulls, too?" I asked.

"No. We're going to have a museum," he said. "It will be a pigeon and dove center. Doves symbolize so many things."

"Around here they mainly symbolize dove season, which starts next week, I think."

He looked at me closely.

"You know, I think I'm falling in love with you," he said.

How strange. But it wasn't as strange as what happened later. I came home one day to find two crates of pigeons awaiting me on my front porch, with a note which read: "If you want to see me again, let the blue ones fly, but if you never want to see me again, let the red ones go."

They all looked the same to me. They looked like standard pigeons—gray feathers with white little bellies. So, I let them all go. When he called me with a few questions about the arrival of all his pigeons at the same time, I told him, "My answer is this: I WON'T PLAY YOUR GAMES."

That didn't do much good. He kept hounding me for about two more years. I suppose he had a hard time with rejection, and an easy time with stalking. Sometimes I think I see him parked on the corner near my house in order to watch my comings and goings.

"PigeonMan" was quite annoying, but the pigeons themselves were worse. They left a trail of droppings and feathers on the porch that were almost impossible to clean up. I could sympathize with city dwellers who considered them "flying rats."

At least PigeonMan didn't have a criminal record, as far as I knew. I couldn't say as much for some of my other "amatory interests." For example, there was Huevos, the car thief, who proudly regaled me with the story of his exploits in the field of wealth redistribution.

"You were stealing cars?" I asked, horrified.

"Yes. In Dallas. You didn't know? I was famous for it." He was actually proud of it.

"Hmm. You weren't all that famous," I responded. I paused before continuing. "And, why was it such a big deal to steal cars in Dallas?"

"I stole them to give them to the poor. I was the 'Cowboy Robin Hood,'" he said.

"How ridiculous!" I looked at him wondering what he had that caused me to be interested in him. What could it be? Was I just hopelessly attracted to felons and weirdos? The answer seemed to be a very obvious YES. He had what it took to catch my eye: a picaresque life, absurd, illogical—that was what drew me in. It wasn't his success that fascinated me, it was his utter failure due to his grandiosity. His life was madness, utter madness. So, I plunged headlong into some sort of potentially unhealthy intellectual romance. But, the cute little picaresque adventure didn't last long. The police arrested him and, when I refused to lend him $5,000 to post bail, he got mad. After that, he wouldn't even let me see him in jail. How disappointing.

Perhaps one day he might have understood why I looked at him in the same manner I once counted the amoeba in a drop of pond water. He wasn't something from a 10th-grade biology class, though.

And then I moved to Paraguay. I went there to study the rhetorical strategies used in promoting democracy after a 35-year-old dictatorship. The task was overwhelming. How do you measure the impact of a free press and freedom of expression when, for 35 years, there were paid informants listening in at all public gatherings and on all telephone conversations?

The same thing happened in Uruguay, and there various individuals had estimated it took approximately 5 months for writers to develop a chronic and possibly incurable case of self-censorship.

In my case, I had always secretly hoped that studying propaganda would lead to the ability to generate diabolically effective propaganda for my own sordid uses.

So far, no luck. Perhaps it was because I hadn't quite decided on what my "sordid uses" might be. Perhaps I would find some in Paraguay.

★ ★ ★

It was late November. The season changed from hot and muggy to hotter and muggier, and people started to talk about how even the streets were melting in Asunción. I found that hard to believe, since they were mainly cobblestone, but it was a nice idea.

I kept thinking about Tia Erqueminia, and I couldn't get her out of my mind. I had a feeling that she was right, but when I confronted my fiancé, he denied it all. "Of course there's no one else! You're the only woman I want!"

But it wasn't enough.

"My problem is that I'm not shallow and empty enough," I said.

I was explaining my new theory about my disasters with men to a new friend who had just invited me to go with him to Iguazu, and to see the waterfalls and dams of Itaipu.

We were drinking coffee and eating pastry at "El Molino" (the mill).

"I thought you were just a friend," I said. "Why are you inviting me to go to Ciudad del Este with you? What do you plan to do with your wife? Won't she complain? Or do you have a big trunk?"

"Look, don't be a fool. My wife and I are separated. It's been that way for years. She married me only because she had heard rumors that fertility doctors always called me when the sperm banks were running low, or when there were a number of withdrawals."

"All premature, I suppose," I said slyly.

He glowered at me.

"You're not shallow—you're a vast wasteland of femininity. Didn't your mother teach you anything?" he asked.

"Absolutely not. I am a product of my era and of my friends. Well, my esteemed companion, many thanks for the coffee and the conversation. I've got to go."

I left El Molino feeling a little gruff and very frustrated. Where on earth could anyone find any respect these days? Respect. The person who wants respect has to enforce it, is what my mother always

told me. But, how? That's the first question. And what do men re-
spect anyway? Pretty legs, a nice ass, a domesticated demeanor. If that
were the case, what kind of animal was I?

"Move it, pig!"

I didn't realize I was standing dead in my tracks on the corner
without paying attention to the traffic noise and the people who sur-
rounded me.

"Pig? Thanks! I was wondering what I was—" I shouted back. The
guy who yelled at me stared at me as if I were from another planet.

"Stupid clown!" he said.

Maybe I should lose weight and not use so much makeup, I re-
flected. Or, maybe not. It's not that I'm fat or skinny or that I'm a
tacky dresser. It's that I'm a woman, and for women, it's easy to make
ourselves victims, if we travel alone without protection. And it's not
even necessary to go around with messy hair, badly-painted nails, and
dishevelled clothes. It's not necessary to lower oneself to the level of
actually getting dirty—what's important is leaving the impression of
being untouchable—a pariah. What a shame that I had at least some
shred of human dignity left. Of course that shred wasn't enough to
defend myself, but it was more than enough to immerse myself in
anthropological investigation.

It already seems to me that someone plunged me into some sort
of weird field study without my permission, and now I have to take
notes on the de-evolution of the homo-sapiens brain. It is not a
pretty sight. And, the whole time, I'm realizing that instead of learn-
ing to adapt and survive, I spent years and years at the university
learning to lose all my normal self-preserving instincts. How do you
like that? Instead of using my education to break the stereotype of
the defenseless woman, I'm an exaggeration of that—maybe even a
thousand times worse for my ability to delude myself that my educa-
tion was worth something.

Propaganda. If only I could generate it and use it for myself.

* * *

I was looking in the refrigerator one cold December night. I was
reading the work of Mussolini's speechwriters and I was feeling quite
hungry and bleary-eyed. There was nothing left in the refrigerator but
one can of Diet Pepsi and the hideous skeleton of my Thanksgiving

turkey. Shreds of desiccated meat clung to the bones, and a layer of yellowish gelatin shimmered on the bottom of the pan. I wondered if my beagle would eat it, and if he did, if it would cause him to choke. At least it would stop his incessant baying when the neighborhood cats taunted him from the top of the wooden stockade fence. If it didn't choke him, it would give him diarrhea, I concluded, and I heaved the strangely smell-less cadaver into a Hefty trash bag with drawstring neck.

The phone rang. The turkey bones creaked as I startled. The shrivelled meat made a sound like a woman whacking a hambone against a kitchen table.

"Hey baby, why don't you come to my apartment so I can explore the outer reaches of the cosmos?"

"What? Do what? Who's speaking?"

"Don't you recognize my voice? It's your ex speaking."

"What ex? I don't have an ex—I have a dull, boring single life and have had for years. Thanks to animals like you."

Unfortunately, my mysterious caller wasn't near enough for me to offer him a turkey (bone) sandwich. He was certainly not in any danger of choking on a bone.

"I miss you. A lot."

"Your voice sounds strange. Have you been drinking?" I asked.

"Oh, a little, I guess. Me and my buddy just got back from Valley of the Dolls."

"A topless dancing place?"

"There were a lot of really pretty women. They made me think of you. Why don't you come over? I love you a lot. Really."

"Oh, really. Suddenly you miss me after going to a trashy nude dancing place."

"It wasn't all that trashy."

"Don't call me! Do you understand? And I'm going to leave the phone off the hook."

What a life. What a lack of respect. At times, I think that for having been born a woman, in an era so confusing, it's my destiny to learn how to fake loving the role of the "liberated" woman while I look at the absolute lack of support and understanding of those around me. But isn't it a little ridiculous to want more? If I don't understand myself, how can anyone else hope to understand me?

TIA ERQUEMINIA

I began to lose myself in a daydream of how it would be if I were married.

"I'm telling you, honey, I'm sick of hearing you beg me to fix you something from the deer you slaughtered on your stupid hunting trip. You know very well that if it doesn't come packaged for the microwave, I won't be able to fix it."

In the vast landscape that my imagination produced, my kitchen was filled with books, none with recipes but books on philosophy and dictionaries. Occasionally, a page or two from those books would catch on fire for being to close to the stove. That always bugged me. I didn't want to lose my books to fire. I preferred to burn the meat. And what about that subject—burning the meat?

From the depths of my imagination, the voice of my supposed husband called me: "Don't tell me that you're microwaving the venison in a metal dish, dear! Please, tell me no! What has happened to you?"

"I like the little lightning bolts that come from the can," I replied. "Next, I'm throwing in the cat."

"What?" he said. Obviously the American urban myth about exploding cats and poodles in the microwave hadn't made its way into his skull. Neither had the phenomenon of the Miss Havisham's Kitchen—something I dubbed after Charles Dicken's *Great Expectations*, Miss Havisham being the old crone who refused to change out of her wedding gown and clear out the wedding cake after her husband-to-be stood her up at their wedding. Fifty years later, she was still wearing the now-ragged wedding dress and rats were running in and out of the cobweb-infested cake.

In Paraguay, no one understood my aversion to the kitchen. They understood my jokes and ironic commentary even less.

"Don't feel you have to defrost your freezer on my account," I said to my fiancé's mother, who was directing the empleada to clean out the freezer while we sipped coffee and munched on petit-fours. "I have some packages of green beans that have been in my freezer for seven years. The green beans now resemble creatures that have not been found on Planet Earth since the Devonian."

I could tell by her face that she thought I must be joking. I wasn't. I needed to punt—and fast.

"Aahh, hah-hah—just a joke! Just wanted you to know that you

111

don't have to be perfect around me," I said.

"I already knew that," she said. "THAT was more than obvious."

She was laughing, and I knew she liked me, but I felt miserable and misunderstood. Our senses of irony made only the most tangential contact, and so the joy of communication was tenuous and ephemeral at best.

It was a hot, steamy Paraguayan afternoon. It had rained earlier, and the streets were wet. In the distance, I could still hear thunder rumbling and I wondered if we were in for more rain.

I was standing on the corner near the monument to the Heroes of the Chaco, the war that decimated the male population only 50 years after a different war, the War of the Triple Alliance, wiped out almost all the male population. Why commemorate slaughter? I thought cynically. Or war itself for that matter?

It made it seem as though a state of war were preferable to peace. No one ever constructs monuments to the peaceable ones, during the peaceable years.

Many war survivors have had a hard time adjusting to peace, not so much due to their wrecked homes, burned-out lives, but because the anarchy and chaos of wartime is supplanted by an unworkable rigidity, a social order that quickly sinks into social control. Dystopia is a type of utopia for the spirit that craves to be free, although the shadow of death, prisoner of war camps, bombings, and fear seem to be quite antithetical to freedom. According to the immortal Rousseau, we were all born free, but, everywhere around us, man is in chains. Here in Paraguay, I had the sense that, for all their protestations to the contrary, the Paraguayan spirit craved war—not for the carnage, not for the slaughter—but for the chance to break free of the rigid social control that the Spanish encomienda system left as a crushing legacy. Che Guevara merely articulated what was on everyone's mind, but unarticulated, unbroadcast. Could I relate to the stereotypical guerrilla freedom fighter?

No. Most definitely not. I was more fascinated by the relics of fascism that goose-stepped about in the Paraguayan psyche.

★   ★   ★

"Who's that?" I asked my fiancé. We were watching television at his house and a vast throng waving red flags chanted and roared at the feet of what appeared to be a rather petite man standing on a raised platform. He was wearing a red gaucho-style scarf and appeared very military.

"That's the general who led the coup against General Stroessner. He's running for president," said my fiancé.

"It's a scene straight out of a Nazi propaganda film," I said. "Look at the panning shots, the medium close-ups, the establishing shot—what's his name, anyway?"

"Nido de Ovejas. He studied in Germany for many years. He's very well-prepared to rule."

"Obviously," I said. I listened to Nido de Ovejas's words. The general was talking law and order.

"I promise to reinstate the death penalty!" he was saying. "I'll use it like they use it in the United States—I'll fry the delinquents!"

He made my flesh crawl. Nido de Ovejas filled my mind with ghastly images of brains exploding and flames flashing out from the skull. I was fascinated.

"Use it like in the United States? That's a GOOD thing?" I asked, incredulously.

"Hey. Don't ask me. I think the guy could be dangerous," said my fiancé.

"I'd love to meet the campaign manager—find out how they're working the images and symbols," I said.

"That can be arranged. But are you sure?" he asked.

"Definitely."

The next day we drove out to Paraguari, about 100 miles east of Asunción, to a country estate in an area of hot springs and rocky hills. General Nido de Ovejas's campaign manager was a dapper man who had a ranch with 20,000 head of cattle and a furniture factory. I wondered how he had time to run the campaign, and assemble 60,000 people.

"It's nice to meet a film expert from the United States," he said to me.

"I'm not really a film expert, although I've studied film. I'm a scholar of propaganda—not advertising so much, although that interests me. I study the propaganda mainly used in war and ideological battles—my specialty is the propaganda of World War II and the early Cold War."

"And you can tell me something about our campaign?" he asked me. We were sitting next to a rock cliff from which a natural waterfall cascaded down into a pool. A modest stone house was next to it, and the smell of carne asada wafted through the torpid afternoon air. I sat politely and sweated like a pig.

"Yes. It's brilliant. But your films have a few flaws. Study Leni Rieftenstahl. She was Hitler's filmmaker. Her films of the Olympics and of Hitler are masterpieces. And, of course, Hitler's rhetoric—"

"Yes, yes, we know all about Hitler's speeches," he said impatiently. "We've been studying the American presidential campaigns, too. Especially the year that Dukakis was running for president."

"It's too bad Lee Atwater's dead," I said. He would have been perfect for Nido de Ovejas.

"Who's Lee Atwater?" he asked. I described Lee Atwater and the Willie Horton revolving door campaign ad. The campaign manager was silent for a moment, obviously contemplating the situation. "Yes, Lee Atwater would have been the perfect person for us."

My fiancé and I drove back to Asunción in silence. The air was thick with humidity and the smell of diesel exhaust. I suddenly felt quite sad. "I've always wanted to have the chance to practice propaganda, not just study it," I said. "Sometimes I feel my life's been wasted—I haven't known what directions to go, and I've just stumbled around in the dark. Why couldn't I have done something?"

"Don't worry," he said. "We'll do great things together."

"Do you think General Nido de Ovejas will call me?" I asked hopefully. "I could tell him how to manipulate the masses more effectively with his campaign promises—how to make the opposition look ridiculous."

"He might call. But he might not. He's very busy," said my fiancé. We drove the rest of the way in silence. In the dark, I felt hot, wet tears slide down my cheeks. I had no idea why I was crying, but I was.

★ ★ ★

"He committed suicide from watching too much Elvis," he said.

We were hanging about the lobby of the Pastos de Paz (Peaceful Pastures) funeral home, sipping espresso that the waiter had given us, and talking about the deceased. This was the eighth or ninth wake I had been to in six months, and I was getting pretty desensitized to it all. At the first Paraguayan wake I attended I started to faint when I saw the body across the room. This time they rolled the open casket right by me, and I didn't even feel nauseous or dizzy. I actually felt a vague stir of curiosity when I saw they had styled the deceased's hair in a '50s-style pompadour.

"Yeah? Well, that will do it all right," I remarked. "I never could understand Elvis worship."

"Toward the end, he watched Elvis movies all day, and wouldn't leave the house. I feel responsible because I brought him those videos from the U.S."

"How tragic. How did he die?"

"He shot himself."

"Did they find peanut butter and banana sandwich in his mouth?" I asked.

"No. He put the gun in his mouth," said my fiancé.

"Oh." I decided it would be best for me to be quiet.

"Yeah, I was hoping that some day he'd invest in a deal with me," said my fiancé, wistfully. "We were going to start talking about that, and then this happened..." His face looked quite grief-stricken.

The source of his discomfort was pretty transparent, I thought. It's good to have friends, isn't it?

★   ★   ★

Tia Erqueminia was doing her nails when I went to her storefront reading room.

"That's a nice shade of purple," I said. "Do you have time to do a reading?"

"Sure, always for you, dear," she said. She started shuffling cards. It was amazing. She didn't even once muss her nails.

"I see you've been sad. Very sad. And you're still sad," she said.

"Uh, yes. But I want to know something I don't already know," I said.

"You've been in bad shape, but no one has any idea," she said. "You've even been thinking about ending your life."

I nodded my head in affirmation. Tears started to splash down off my cheeks and onto my trembling hands.

"The cards never lie," she said. She studied the cards before continuing. "You're going to go on a journey. A long, hard journey. But although your destination is far away, where you're going is where you need to be."

"That's not what I want to hear," I said. "I want to know something good, something positive."

"I don't want to lie to you, dear," she said. "This is just not an easy incarnation for you. You're working out a lot of karma, a lot of bad debt."

"How? What did I do?" I asked.

"You were stupid. You believed men." I looked at Tia Erqueminia very closely. I wondered why she always had such terrible things to say to me. Was she trying to drive me out of the country? Did she have some sort of ulterior motive, or vested interest? I looked at her again. No. Probably not. She just saw that I'd pay for negative readings, but I wasn't too interested in the positive ones. That was my problem, not hers.

I walked back to the apartment I had been leasing while I tried to see if there were any opportunities for me in Paraguay, any manner of earning a living. It was clouding up, and it looked like it would start raining again. I could leave most of my things behind, I thought. Clothes, knick-knacky items, kitchen utensils. I didn't want any reminders, anyway. I'd take my books and my laptop computer and printer. That would be enough.

Too bad I'd be leaving before I'd have the chance to see if Tia Erqueminia's prediction that I'd receive a huge fake diamond cubic zirconium ring would turn out to be true.

* * *

"Hola, hola—where are you?" he asked. We had a bad connection.

"I'm in Dallas. I'm waiting for my connection."

"Dallas? Why?"

"I'm going home. My time's up and I need to get back."

"But what about me? Aren't we going to get married?" he asked.

"Uhh, yes, no, I don't know—maybe," I said.

"My mother and aunt were expecting you for the birthday party next week."

"Could you apologize for me and tell them I won't be able to make it?" I asked.

"Won't you tell me anything?"

"Go see Tia Erqueminia," I said. "She'll explain it all."

"Who?"

"Tia Erqueminia."

"Where is she?" he asked. I told him quickly, then became un-comfortable.

"They're calling my flight. Talk to you later—"

Tia Erqueminia would set him straight. Meanwhile, I wanted to study the propaganda and speeches of Peronist Argentina. That would keep me busy for a few years.

My Hairshirt Has Fleas

It was the morning I had to drive to Dallas and back in a day, and I was feeling nervous and edgy.

That, of course, led to bad nerves, bad communication, and a good, knock-down, drag-out screaming and shouting match.

"You play games!" Doug said, and I shouted back, "Yes, I do!"

Doug was my ex-husband, but we'd been thinking about getting married again. He was my second husband. My first husband was Doug's grandfather. Yeah, I know that sounds weird. We met after my first husband's funeral. Doug was the only one of my in-laws who didn't accuse me of marrying for money. Percival Van Horn Beden was the founder of Longhorn Oil, one of the first companies in West Texas to understand the value of secondary recovery. Under his guidance, he and his Wall Street investors purchased old oil wells in the Permian Basin. It was funny, really. The sellers thought they had gotten the best of a consortium of annoying New Yorkers, when in fact, Beden got the best of them. His company set up injection wells and got the old wells pumping again. He made millions. Even more impressive, he multiplied his millions in real estate and Gulf Coast platform drilling.

No one understood that I actually loved Percival—I loved him because he was good to me and because he would never hurt me. Of course, he was quite frail and he could never physically hurt me—perhaps that was what gave me the self-confidence to trust a man. Percival was a dear, sweet man. He was 89 when we married. I was 24. He died only 9 months later. I was devastated. Then I met Doug and the pain went away temporarily. Doug seemed shy and wise—a younger,

more tender version of Percival. I fell instantly in love with Doug.
Doug seemed to love me in the same way that Percival did.

After awhile I began to suspect I was wrong. Doug wasn't much
like Percival at all. For one, Doug was capable of sex. He even seemed
to want sex. Despite my breast implants (provided by Percival) and
cosmetic surgery, I wasn't much interested in sex. Sure, I like ro-
mance, but I panic at sex. I also like attention. Just don't touch me.
Please.

I had doubts. Had Doug been commissioned by the family to
marry me? Was it a trick? Was it a game? I missed Percival more than
I could even begin to describe.

Doug was looking at me. He said, "Sarabeth, listen to me. You're
paranoid. You exaggerate. You get hysterical!" And I screamed, "Yes,
I do!"

He said, "You're evasive. You won't answer my questions. You mis-
represent the truth to me." I was dying inside, but he didn't know it.
I didn't know it either. All I knew was that I was in pain. He didn't
love me any more. He didn't trust me. He had hardened himself
against me—all because we had rushed into things, marrying after
dating for five weeks—and I had panicked and run away.

But, who wouldn't panic? The lawsuits had started—Percival's
family was trying to take away what I was left in the will. Worse than
that, they were trying to take back the gifts he gave me while we
were dating—the ranch in west Texas, the jewelry, even the little
business he started for me—Sarabeth's Special Secrets—my little lin-
gerie store, which was a naughty version of Victoria's Secret.

Now, after a year with Percival, I had begun to feel a profound
and true love for him. It wasn't infatuation—it was something that
had built over time and tears. But, I knew it was too late.

And now, Doug was asking me questions in the harsh voice he
used when he was disgusted with me. He said he wanted answers. I
didn't have any. I missed Percival—he had never pressured me or made
me feel sad, threatened and alone. Instead, I would look at Percival—
especially in those final months when he was bedridden and termi-
nally ill from prostate cancer—and I'd think about how terrible those
moments must be, knowing you're done for, alone and without allies.
I think Percival, in facing his terminal illness, understood a little of
the abject fear and pain of the victim of childhood sexual abuse.

Doug didn't understand it at all—he was much too healthy and virile. He took my behavior as something directed at him, and he wanted satisfaction. I couldn't give it to him. Only fate and bad luck could give him that knowledge. I felt cornered and desperate.

"The more you ask me, the less I'll say," I said. "So just leave me alone." I slammed the door and walked out of the room.

You could say I had lost my mind, but I hadn't clued in yet. Too bad someone didn't let me know before I became a menace to society.

The problem was that he had grown cold to me and that made me a little wacked. I couldn't face his coldness and it made me act out all the hideous things he accused me of. He saw my sin as that of being a mercenary, cold woman who could not tolerate any sexual contact. He couldn't forgive that and I couldn't tolerate his lack of forgiveness. I knew my sin to be that of running—running from my emotions—running from the sadness at losing the only man who had never pressured me for anything, who only wanted to give, not TAKE TAKE TAKE. Of course, that made no sense to anyone but myself. My family thought I had lost my mind when I married Percival. They didn't know how much I loved him and how good he was to me.

The breast implants were perhaps the most precious of his gifts. Laugh all you want at that one—but hear me out. With my big, beautiful, brazen breasts I had the kind of armor I'd needed all my life. They shouted out my arrivals and departures, and they demanded, "See me! Love me! Feed me! Worship me!" My new tits were armed and dangerous. My new tits took hostages and demanded ransom. Anyone who minded taking a back seat to The Breasts might as well leave before they got good and worked up.

With Bombshell Boobs, I was in control—no one could see shy, ordinary-chested me and think I'd be unquestioning and grateful for their attention. No one would look at me and automatically assume that I'd be so thrilled at any male attention that I'd overlook their cruel little games. Catch the snatch. Bone the dog. You know how they go—prey upon society's throwaways, then you can have your fun and no one will notice.

Percival changed all that.

But he was gone and I had lost my mind.

But, it wasn't all that obvious—to the outside world, I was functioning quite well. The gossip around me—my marrying Percival, then marrying and divorcing his grandson—was free publicity for my store. It got around that I was always in the store and that anyone could have a picture taken with me—I didn't mind. My customers loved me.

It was a good thing they couldn't read my thoughts. I was really wacked. Gone, baby. Completely and literally out of my skull.

At night the madness began. I thought Doug had trapped me and how he was going to pull the old Hanoi Hilton routine on me, I thought. "You're going to feed me rat-foot soup and stick electrodes up my vagina!" I screamed at him one morning. I couldn't understand the sad look on his face. "You're making fun of me!" I hissed at him.

Sometimes I wondered if my hysteria was simply a way to avoid the truth—that I felt incredibly guilty and filled with shame for being so afraid of being loved that I would drive him away.

I had nightmares—dreams of Percival crying in his sleep because of my betrayal. "Sarabeth, I left you enough money so that no man would ever hurt you again. But, you're just begging to be hurt. Can't you see you're doing it to yourself now?"

He was right. With Percival, I never had to endure sex. I never had to be touched. I finally felt safe—and now I was throwing it all away.

It was too much, finally, and I ran away. Then I divorced Doug without telling him. To Doug, it didn't make any sense at all—we were making love one day, divorced the next. What was wrong with me? What was I thinking? Why was I acting this way?

I didn't have any answers.

All I knew was that I couldn't live without him. So, even though he was a still miffed at my secretly divorcing him, Doug and I were giving it another shot. For Doug to even speak to me again meant that he was either a brilliantly wise, enlightened being, or an utter fool—a masochistic glutton for the whip and the cattle prod.

But, maybe our relationship had a chance of working. My guilt would heal all wounds.

It was all my fault, I said.

Was this a manipulative lie, too? Could I tolerate being loved? In my deepest heart of hearts, I didn't know. I had no idea.

"It wasn't all you fault, Sarabeth," said my sister. "Don't you remember how you felt pressured? Don't you remember telling me how you didn't want to move so fast, but you were afraid of losing him? Remember how much you missed Percival—I thought you were going to lose your mind."

The first time I was in Percival's house, he showed me his collection of old stock certificates—most were of oil companies who had started up at the time when Spindletop and the big salt domes were found in Texas. Not many were legitimate companies—the gaudier the certificate, the bigger the scam. Uncle Sam Oil Company was my favorite. It was broke within a year, Percival told me. I liked Magnolia Oil, too. It became Getty Oil, he explained.

It was that first night with Percival that I played my Dumb Bimbo act for him. I had played it many times—when I used it on other people, the routine led to boring conversations, patronizing remarks, cheap wine, and the kind of woozy feeling you get when you're walking on the edge of a water-logged, slime-covered sinkhole. But at least it was followed up with apologies in the morning and a tasteful gift of some sort by nightfall.

But Percival laughed at the act—no—he laughed to see me acting the act. He caught the smirk behind my pouty lips, big mirror-ball earrings, *Blonde Venus* hair, and my *Big Girls Don't Cry* eyes.

I remembered the agony I felt when Percival was gone. Now I was in agony because Doug was gone—not dead, but hardened against me.

It was the story of my life. No one would ever love me unless I worked like hell at it—I let myself become their object. I let them have their way with me. Either that, or I bluffed and faked my way into it. If I molded myself into exactly the person they wanted to see, maybe I'd buy a little affection. But, it was false, and I knew it.

That knowledge was killing me.

★ ★ ★

A few months ago, I became obsessed with movies. Every night, I would sneak to the neighborhood video store and rent all the black widow, or praying-mantis-who-always-eats-her-mate movies I could find. The list was long—*Black Widow, Fatal Attraction, Double Indemnity, The Postman Always Rings Twice, Gilda, Basic Instinct, Sunset Boulevard.*

The list of weird lines and pathologies they were giving me was long, too.

One night, Doug and I were eating pesto on whole wheat pasta and drinking a California cabernet. I looked him straight in the eye and made a pronouncement.

"I've given up games. I'm only interested in the truth." Doug looked unconvinced. Actually, so was I. How could I give up games when I couldn't even tell when I was playing?

We were watching the classic *The Blue Angel*, which had been filmed during the decadent post-WWI Weimar Republic years. Marlene Dietrich was doing her cabaret act and bringing about the ruination of her husband, the lonely former professor.

"Watch out for blondes—there's something special about them— a little flirting is all right, but remember they're predators," sang Marlene, the tantalizing Lola-Lola.

I despised myself. Was I some sort of cheap, aging Lola-Lola?

"Truth is a magician's assistant," I said, daydreaming in tandem with the unfolding narrative of the film.

"Why do you say that?" he asked.

"What?" I said, startled. I wasn't listening to him. I had only been repeating something Percival had said to me once. He saw truth as a moving target—the closer you got to it, the more it moved away. Percival used to smile at my evasiveness, my compulsive lying, and he'd look at me with incredibly sad and understanding eyes. He understood. He lied to everyone about his illness—no one but his doctors and I knew it was prostate cancer. He said it was heart disease. His death certificate would say heart attack. He had already made certain of that.

Doug would never know what I was really thinking—about how afraid I was to let him know how much I longed for him to love me in the same gentle, patient, and tolerant way as Percival. Doug's body was gorgeous—Percival's was not. But both had gentle faces and warm, caring, forgiving essences that I needed more than anything else in this world. But Doug could never love me, I thought to myself. I'm worthless. What could he see in me? I might as well push him away before he sees the light and dumps me so fast I don't even feel the sensation of falling—I just feel my gut smacking into the earth.

You would never guess that was what was going on if you simply looked at me.

Fear of being vulnerable—being rejected—made me start paying attention again—I imagined how my words might sound in a script and how my actions might appear on screen. One night, I angled my face to Doug in what I imagined gave me a vulnerable yet tormented look.

"I was afraid of you. You're insane. You're violent," I said. I was stabbing the sharpened tip of a pen into my pantyhose and making even little shreddings all around my knees and calves.

"The truth is that I've been afraid of you because I thought what you did that first night was rape," I continued. "You had your way with me. You're violent."

I looked at Doug to see how he was reacting. Although I thought I was in control and playing a game, the only game I was playing was with myself. The problem was, I had worked myself up into believing the "Night At the Drive-In" video store melodrama I was enacting.

Forget actually telling him I suspected that his family put him up to marry me—put him up to hooking me so I'd have to give back the things Percival gave me. It was so ridiculous—how could they be so greedy? After all, Percival had been worth around $500 million. All that he gave me added up to less than $2 million. Why did they care?

Doug looked at me oddly.

"That's crazy. I'm the gentlest person I know," he said. "I didn't rape you."

I knew it, but if it had happened, perhaps it would explain the friction and my mistrust of him. Wasn't it better to believe in the "plausible explanation"? That always made more sense that real life, anyway.

If he only married me to control me, he had raped me—physically and emotionally.

"You forced me!" I shouted again. That's what I'd started believing. Funny, I didn't even think of the actual date rape that had happened almost five years ago—maybe because it was so pathetically typical, straight out of a *Mademoiselle* or *Good Housekeeping* article.

"Why did you leave me?" Doug asked.

"I had to leave you. I believed you were a monster. And, you were—don't you see it?" I asked.

"No. You were wrong," he said.

This was going nowhere. *The Blue Angel* was still going on the VCR. Professor Unrath was putting on his clown suit. He looked beaten, demented.

"I've got to go." I was half-listening to the film. "An egg. A real egg. A man. A real man. What I want is a real man." I thought of the singing and dialogue from *The Blue Angel* as Professor Unrath was driven mad by the torments of his wife.

"Where are you going?" Doug asked. The Witness Stand again. This was not going as I wanted it to. I tried to make my eyes look glazed and unblinking. Percival would never have done this. He was always sweet. He was always good to me—he was the only man in the world who would or could appreciate me. Why did I think Doug would be able to do that? Doug was decades away from the wisdom of Percival.

"Where are you going?"

"Why do you want to know?" I responded. "It's for work. I'll be gone for a day. Why does it matter?" I said.

"You're being evasive again," he said.

On the screen, Professor Unrath was reaching for Lola-Lola's throat. A recent biography of Marlene Dietrich explained that the game was not a game, acting was not acting. The actor, Emil Jannings, who played Professor Unrath was jealous of Dietrich and badly bruised her throat in the throttling scene. Doug looked at the screen and stared at me.

"You're doing it again. You're playing games!" he shouted at me.

I grabbed the bag with my laptop computer, maps, and directions to the north Dallas restaurant I was thinking about buying. I could feel the air whipping my bare knees where the pantyhose flapped in ruins around them.

"Then stop questioning me!" I ran out the door.

The week before, the Witness Stand game had dragged on even longer.

"You're leaving?" he asked. It always started the same. "I've got to run errands." "What kind of errands?" "Really boring ones—it won't take too long, but I'm dreading it."

"Why don't you answer my questions?" he asked. "What do you want—a detailed description?" I asked.

At this point, we had been divorced as long as we had been married—four months—but the emotional stranglehold we had on each other now was much tighter and more lethal than anything we had experienced while we were married.

What I was doing was none of his business. Why did he want to know? He was constantly asking me to define myself, my business, my relationship to him. He asked questions about Percival. I wouldn't tell him.

Just to throw him off track, I defined myself to him in a different way every time he asked. Why don't you trust me? he asked. Why should I? I always asked him that at the end of the argument. I said, Tell me this: Why is it in my best interests to trust you? Let me run a cost-benefit analysis. What makes me think I can trust you? Why do you ask me to trust you?

"Because I love you," he said.

I froze. It was always the same answer. Always the worst possible thing he could say. Right. You love me. All the more reason to destroy me, I thought.

Sure, he was nice to me. Sometimes. More often, he was competitive. He wanted me to admire him, he said. I believed him, as far as that went. But, he had a habit of saying insulting things, then blaming me for provoking them—he was Mr. Perfection, he said. I knew him for his insecurity. Of course, I was no paragon of self-assuredness. Maybe I was the one who was competitive. What did it matter? Who cared anyway?

Well, I guess I did.

We weren't getting anywhere and I didn't understand him. I didn't understand me.

I couldn't let him know.

"Men swarm around me like a moth to a flame—how can I help it if they get burned?" Marlene Dietrich's words echoed in my head. Ah yes, so appropriate that the English version was called *Falling In Love Again*—something to completely catch you off guard.

I was lost, miserable and seeking explanations, and I didn't even know the questions to ask.

* * *

The answers, and the questions, would come on a day that was as hot as a hallucination.

I was going to meet Doug's uncle Mike—the one who had started the lawsuits and, I suspected, put Doug up to marrying me in order to get his hands on the gifts Percival had given me.

According to Percival, Doug's uncle was a "knucklehead and damn fool" who wouldn't stay in college and ended up going to Bolivia where he was a part of a fringe Jehovah's Witness cult that had bought up an old tin-mining town in the Andes and was waiting for the world to end. When it didn't after ten or fifteen years, he returned to Texas. He came back stupid and mean, said Percival.

Why? What happened? I asked. "I don't think it was what happened in the Jehovah's Witnesses. It was something to do with the military. That was during the time of the desaparecidos—the Peronistas were kidnapping anyone they suspected of being a part of the insurgency. A lot of Argentines and American mercenaries were hiding out in Bolivia," said Percival. What did they do to him in Bolivia? Torture? "Yes. And I think they raped him and then let him go. It would have been better to be tortured, then let killed. But, they did something he couldn't ever admit."

"And it was his own damn fault. He was so fired up that he could save the world that he'd believe anyone who fed him a pack of lies." Percival looked sad. "Honey, he should have come home, gotten medical attention, then gotten a job. But he could never admit to anyone what happened. He told me—well, he hinted at it. He could never tell anyone in the family. Later, he hated me because I knew." At that, I started crying. Percival had never been more sweet.

I missed Percival. He was so wise. Doug seemed young, horny and stupid to me sometimes. But, I loved him, even if he was unenlightened.

Sweating in the 104-degree Dallas heat, missing the I-635 exit and not knowing it until halfway past downtown Dallas—"Hey, what's downtown doing here?" then realizing I had missed the turn about 10 miles back. The backtrack would be tedious, especially since I liked to wing it & try for "shortcuts." Devising shortcuts on backroads in an unfamiliar city is not something I could really recommend—yet, every time I looked ahead to a long stretch of dull, sun-bleached, monochromatic road, I did it.

The Metroplex stretched out in front of me. I got on I-30 West, headed toward DFW airport & the towns between Dallas and Fort Worth. Oakcliff. Irving. An abandoned amusement park blistered off on the side of the road. I was driving in a faded, sticky-hot animation cell from The Jetsons. There was an enormous ruined billboard on the side.

B   O   A   D   W   A

Boardwalk? Broadway? I couldn't tell.

Heat waves rose up off the pavement. It was noon. Somewhere in the distance I saw a billboard—a tiny, intense, monastic & self-flagellated Lawrence of Arabia on horseback, whipping up his horse into a foam. It was a part of that ruined Broadway/Boardwalk amusement park.

A mirage rose up. This was even more equivocal and potentially dangerous. It was me, looking at myself gazing into the mirror. I looked balanced, lucid, and calm. Knowing myself, I would say that those sky-blue eyes were signaling the end of another broadcasting day—the end of a stretch of clear weather, the end of a peaceful interlude that someday would provide fodder for cheap nostalgia and an even cheaper bottle of anniversary champagne. "Ah—our first year of marriage—didn't it have some good days. Remember, dear?"

Ah, yes. That first glorious year.

Never mind the wife who got it in her head she had married a cannibalistic ax-murderer, never mind the wife's sudden interest in the Marquis de Sade, never mind the wife's hysterical scenes, "He's trying to kill me—with the SuperSoaker—No, it's not a toy for his nephew—he bought it and now he's going to fill it up with hydrofluoric acid and etch my face like glass!" Was I that wife? Of course not. I was too sad to be hysterical. Or, was I so sad I was always hysterical? I couldn't tell.

Yes, the snags.

I had married a man, filed for divorce four months later, finalized it in another three months, all the while not quite knowing why except my back was up against the wall. Of course, Percival's family thought I was a mercenary little hussy. Was I? They didn't know. I loved Doug, too. Didn't they understand? They called me a slut and a money-grubbing bitch. They thought I fell for Doug's trap because I thought he had money, too, and I would take it from wherever I could get it. Now Doug didn't seem to love me. I was pushed to the limit and I had nowhere to go but into the lurid, paranoid, obsessive thoughts that churned around in my head.

I wasn't the only one with a wild story.

Doug said his uncle told him a story about how a woman once broke his jaw. He said she pulled a gun, stuck it to his head and almost pulled the trigger. Then she smashed his face with the butt-end of the gun. The only thing that stopped her from killing him was the knowledge that she might spend her life in jail. Why'd she do that to him? He was trying to rape her. That was the story, at least. But, Doug's uncle Mike denied everything—he said they had been dating and she indicated she wanted to make love. Her name was Camelia Rosa Delgado. She was from Argentina but she was living in Waco where Mike had ended up after running out of gas on his way to Percival's ranch to hit him up for money.

Percival's son wore a brace on his jaw for three months and stayed drunk the whole time. There were rumors he had started shooting up cheap Mexican heroin. That was the only explanation for his behavior. Percival was horrified by his son. He told him so and said he wouldn't give him any money that would end up in a needle in a vein. Later that month, Mike disappeared one night to join yet another cult, this time one where he could be one of the "Mighty Men" before he got scared and ran away from Ranch Apocalypse two weeks before the other Mighty Men were attacked by federal agents and subjected to a long, long siege before being torched in the Armageddon they said they expected and welcomed. Mike wouldn't talk to Percival. He wrote a couple of letters, and referred to Percival as a "Mighty Man Wannabe." Percival said he just couldn't understand Mike—a guy with all the advantages he never had.

Didn't they make a movie about the dynamics of the family? Didn't they call it *The Wild Bunch*? Or was it *Apocalypse Now*?

Well, at least a stranger broke Mike's jaw. My family accords that honor to its very own. My mother beat me until my spirit was pulp and I began to walk and talk like the zombie I had begun to believe I was. My family—what a movie that would make: *They Eat Their Young*.

How about the other possibilities? *The Bad Seed*? *The Shining*? *The Night Porter*? *The Mosquito Coast*? "It's family tradition. Do it.

Do it. Do it."

Ah, hysteria. What a beautiful, grotesque, surreal, piece of performance. Give me a needle. I'm ready to try heroin now.

What is hysteria? Is it nature or nurture-based? What is tribal and what is bullshit? What is inculcated by the family, and what is invented from tabloid TV?

I played games. I played them on myself. I missed turnoffs and then wondered how that happened. I let "fate" determine my path. Fate was the name I gave absent-mindedness (or disassociation). I never recognized the things that were truly "fate"—bad things usually—That's why I was on this highway now to Arlington to meet the man whose jaw was allegedly broken by a pissed-off 90-pound woman.

I was here because I loved Doug. I loved my husband more than I could ever love anyone—even myself. I loved him and I wanted him back. But, I thought I had lost him. If I couldn't talk to him, at least I could talk to the man who poisoned our chances. I wanted answers.

So, here I was in Dallas—Arlington, to be precise.

The scenery was surprisingly inoffensive and the traffic relatively light. Was this some sort of holiday? Billboards advertising car dealerships, McDonald's, the Dallas Cowboys, and FM radio celebrities broke up the view of tall grass, tree-lined streams, and small lakes. I passed through Oakcliff without incident. There was a ruined industrial area, but it was not harsh in appearance like the northeast. It was difficult to believe that Oakcliff has one of the highest murder rates in Texas. The violence of Texas is masked by the regal shades of bluebonnets and thick, gold grass.

Did I believe the story about Mike? Was he really raped by Argentine fascists who thought he was a mercenary hiding out in Bolivia? Why would he allow a young Argentine woman to break his jaw? What did he do to her? Did I have any right to speculate? That was many years ago (20), and I was not involved in any way—unless I believed sexual violence to be genetically determined. Doug's father (Mike's younger brother) had been obsessed with breeding racing carrier pigeons. Perhaps his obsession was an attempt to control his unholy urges. Who could tell—the family was twisted with jealousy and suspicion. Did Mike bribe Doug to marry me? Did Doug love me or was this a game?

The lawsuits, the suspicion, the lies and allegations—I could feel myself being provoked by Doug's uncle. I was angry with him for suing me to get back Percival's gifts—yes, that was one thing—but I was even angrier at the possibility he bribed or coerced Doug to marry me so he could take away or control any hint or touch of Percival. Did Doug's uncle hate Percival so much? Did Doug secretly hate me so much?

Here I was, working myself up again. My vocabulary created my reality. My words were blueprints for body blows to self and soul. Of course this violence was self-inflicted—the original, precipitating wounds were so far back in my consciousness, and the rage for pain so internalized that I could not even recognize what was happening. I was afraid and I thought there must be a good reason for it.

I turned off at the Arlington exit and stopped at a light. A dog was barking in the back of the pickup in front of me. Two kids were tormenting each other in the backseat of the car next to me.

There were too many questions and too many ambiguities on this 104-degree mirage-ridden day.

★ ★ ★

I exited onto Division Street in Arlington. The heat was truly amazing. It was reflected and magnified in the parking lots, and here I was, pulling over into the closest one—a Denny's—to use the pay phone next to the grass, where humid air boiled up sweat and a bad temper. But I was too road-zoned and AC'd to be in a bad mood. Plus, I knew I was on the edge of a discovery.

What was my game? I fantasized about spinning a gorgeously sticky and dangerous web. Of course, I was the only one who could be stuck on that web. Did you ever see a black widow hung up on her own web?

I dialed 1-411 and asked for the number for the Oasis Motel. Percival had made a joke that after one cult after another, Mike had finally found his oasis, and it was in the Red Light district of Arlington. Hope he gets some pussy, he said. "How do I get to the motel?" The directions were easy. I was only a few blocks from the motel. What a coincidence. You can't tell me that wasn't a miracle, or a sign from the heavens. I called directory assistance again and got Mike's number. I braced myself.

I dialed Mike Beden's number, but I hung up before it rang. I decided to buy a little time and get up my courage to call from the Oasis Motel's pay phone.

The Oasis Motel reminded me of the Traveler's Lodge in Douglas, Arizona, where my sister and I crashed one spring break evening after driving all day in the Sonora Desert which stretched across southeast Arizona and southwest New Mexico. I found sleazy Mexican comic books in the drawers. The paint in the pool was chipped. The tiny bar of Hecho en Mexico jabon (soap) melted to nothingness after about 3 minutes of contact with hot water.

Behind it was a small, rundown neighborhood, where all the windows had bars over them. It was the kind of place where people die of heat exhaustion, but no one finds them until the smell interrupts pimping and crack-dealing at the Oasis.

There were no black widows in these parts, only tarantulas.

But the Douglas Traveler's Lodge wasn't a dangerous place, just rundown—the teddy bear logo was faded, and the rooms threadbare and scented with Lysol. The Oasis Motel was something else. As I drove up, I noticed it was clean enough, but hard-edged. In the office, the owner greeted me from behind bullet-proof glass in the kind of cage you see in Chicago where Transit Authority employees sell subway tokens and hand out maps.

"Do you have a pay phone?" I told the plump Pakistani behind the bullet-proof glass.

I was a furry blonde tarantula whose bite would rot a man's flesh.

"Yes, it's on the wall next to the door outside," he said.

I called the number. I wondered how I would explain that I was Doug's wife, now ex-wife.

I could just imagine how it would go. "Hi, I'm Sarabeth Mayrocker and I've come to bring you the Good News about the Truth and how you can have the Fruits of the Spirit and Joy Everlasting before the Final Conflagration." The Mayrocker would be an improvisation—a made-up last name to keep him on his toes. If he caught on, good for him. If not, maybe he'd open up to the promise of a new Doomsday cult to join. Or, maybe I'd be more sheepish: "Hi. I'm the wife Doug had for four months before I flipped out and started believing he was a child of the devil. I never got the chance to meet you before you filed the lawsuits. It's pointless, and besides, I hate you, but here I am."

It didn't go like that at all. I stood there in awkward silence, shifting my weight on my feet.

My tarantula fantasy was yet another pathetic delusion of grandeur. My arms were blonde, skinny, and hairy. They had no arachnid jointings.

"Uh, hi, I mean, hello—I want to—umm—introduce myself—I'm Sarabeth—I married Doug," was what finally came out of my mouth.

I braced myself to be excoriated for being a nuisance at best, a cold, malicious meddler at worst. The game I thought I was playing evaporated before my eyes. My self-confidence went the same way—like a film of water sprayed over a blistering hot blacktop road.

"Oh yes, Doug told us he had gotten married. Aren't you divorced?" said Mike.

Images of myself flashed in my mind's eye—me, locked in the bathroom, carving crucifixes into the door frame, hyperventilating, intoning over and over "Agonies die, qui tollis peccata mundi, dona eis requiem."

I stared at the concrete block wall the phone was on.

"I'm in Arlington and I'm at the Oasis Motel. I'd like to talk to you, if you don't mind," I said.

I had expected Mike to be at the Oasis, but he wasn't. He had his own place near the Oasis.

"I suppose that would be all right. If you're at the Oasis, you're almost here—my house is next door to it," he said. The caution in his voice alerted me to the fact he didn't trust me, and that he'd only talk to me if he thought he could get me to do what he wanted. No way would I give up what Percival meant for me to have.

The door to the rundown frame house badly in need of paint and new windows was opened by a blonde, haggard echo of Doug.

Mike was a thin, wiry man and he had a worried, tense expression on his face. I tried to imagine him as a Jehovah's Witness or a Mighty Man, but I failed. I tried to imagine him as a charismatic mad messiah. I failed at that, too. Was he raped in Bolivia by Argentine death squads? It was not too hard to imagine.

Where was the monster spawned in the Bolivian Andes when no one was looking? Where was the beast whose jaw was smashed by a betrayed, broken-hearted woman? Where was the monster who hated his grandson so much that he wanted to destroy anything good that the grandfather had left in this world?

This was Percival's grandson—hurt, jealous, petty. Now I wanted to see him suffer for the pain he had caused me.

"I'm sorry about the litigation," said Mike. I startled. That was not what I was expecting to hear. "The probate attorneys said we should do it. As far as I'm concerned, you are entitled to anything Percival gave you—but it does diminish the size of the estate and that's how the attorneys calculate their fees."

I didn't know if what he was saying was true or not. He sat down on the saggy side of an old, massive sofa. On the end table, under a covered wagon-shaped lamp was a Bible and a stack of *Watchtower* magazines. I guess he wasn't completely deprogrammed from the Jehovah's Witnesses. The way he was rather shy, eager to please, and articulate reminded me of Doug.

The family resemblance extended beyond appearance—it was strange to see Doug's gestures and mannerisms in another person. I felt a tug of sadness to be reminded of Doug. Then I saw echoes of Percival in Mike Beden. That hurt most of all.

I chewed on a hangnail, stared at the floor, fought back sudden tears, and cringed at the hideous vulnerability I suddenly felt. I contemplated hiding behind a wildly theatrical and inappropriate outburst.

This was not pleasant. This experience was telling me more about myself and my exaggerations than about Doug. Fuck Doug. Fuck us. Fuck my weak skittish heart. This enlightenment was annoying. I was starting to see Doug as fragile, eager-to-please—anything but the Mr. Hyde creature I had built up in my head. I could see how great-grandfather, grandson, and great-grandson had clashed. Mike was somewhat shy, as if it took every scrap of energy he possessed to flail away demons and unwanted thoughts of paranoia and despair. I imagined that Doug's occasional overconfidence could throw his uncle off balance and into a severe depression.

It was the same sort of defense reaction that made me wish I could be a black widow or a tarantula.

★   ★   ★

Percival was not a messiah. I think he was my salvation, though, even if for only a few months.

Doug would be angry if he knew I was meeting with his uncle. He was still angry about my accusing him of marrying me just to get a pay-off from his family.

Would Mike ever stop going from Doomsday cult to Doomsday cult? Would he ever stop setting himself up to be raped, fucked over, then cast into semi-poverty and isolation? Would Mike ever realize that it wasn't his father that made him feel like a creature from another planet—he was doing it to himself? It would be difficult. Percival was dead, and yet the wake he left in his path was more powerful than ever. You couldn't help but be swept away. I thought of my own father, and my problematic relationship with him. It would be difficult for me, if I were in his situation. What? I was in his situation. It was tough. There was no question of that. Would I ever be able to break away?

Yes, but only if I switched Doomsday cults—I'd have to jettison the one I was in for this one. Oh well, why not. A television and a Bible are much better than the 365,000-mile GMC Jimmy all rigged up with wires and crystals.

My dad refused to stay in one place—he roamed the continental U.S. in the 4-wheel-drive vehicle the manufacturer advertised as recreational, but in his hands, converted to anything but that, unless you consider it somehow fun to become utterly possessed by the demon of hunger, pain, and starvation that masquerades as a 100-million barrel oil field conjured up out of barren rock and salt water. A click of the machine, a twitch of the rod & you're gone for good—lost in a land of eternal searching for what can never be found.

His dad refused to stay in one place for very long—he was searching for the perfect oasis of pain, the place where artesian springs bubbled up a mad messiah or two to supplant the big one—Percival—who was as unfightable in death as in life. Torture and possible rape at the hands of Argentine fascists only made Percival's hold on Mike grow even tighter. Mike's oasis was, transparently, a peeling frame house. Maybe a sofa with a pile of *Watchtower* magazines on the end table.

The streets in Arlington need to be renamed. Let's not mess with Division Street. Let's just go with the theme it proposes. Rupture

Boulevard. Fragmentation Lane. Fraction Heights. Shattered Drive. Scatter Road. Deconstruction Avenue. Broken Way.

The road home will be rough. I'm not about to set out yet. Mike looked at me curiously. I realized I'll be going alone. He's on his own trail. "These eight years have been hard, really tough. God is punishing me." I imagine a man in his 40s, eight years celibate. I can't imagine it. Is masturbation allowed? Of course not.

Doug says his mother bursts into tears when she thinks about the way her brother's life has been wasted. I try not to fall into that trap. Who's to say it's been wasted? Mike told me that for the last eight years, he's been developing a code book for life. "What do you mean?" I asked him. "It explains everything. Why the big M in McDonald's is yellow. What the frequency of the McDonald's M does to people who see it. Why street signs never quite line up to the streets—they either hover over them or are off to one side. What looking at the white line in the middle of the Interstate will do to your brain and why the U.S. is the only country in the world with that lane marker pattern."

All I could say was, "Oh. Cool." I thought of Percival calling Mike a "knucklehead and a damn fool" and I almost started laughing. What this man needed was a piece of ass. Not my ass, mind you. His energies were misdirected.

Wasted lives. My dad—spending 20 years on an invention that has made him the laughing stock of his cohorts.

Whose yardstick are you using? My yardstick has always measured life in calories expended.

Like my mom, with her thin, thin elegance—she wasted her anorexic accomplishments of haute couture emaciation by spending years in a darkened room with tangled hair and a sinus headache. Wasted, wasted, wasted.

The faster and longer I run on the hamster wheel the better I am. That's what I tell myself. But, after a long, hard year of the high-pitched squeal of unlubricated metal wire turning around in circle after circle, I'm in the same place I was when I started. My muscles are sore, I've stuffed my cheekpouches with sunflower seeds, and my ears are ringing with the incessant whine of directionless activity.

The incessant whine of my dad's invention that detects oil, gas, gold, silver, even treasure. The ringing of shovels against hard-packed dirt as he and his treasure-hunting buddy dig all day in an abandoned barn after getting a TREASURE reading on the Scanner in what they claim was old Shawnee Chief Billy Bowlegs' buried gold coins and paper money. Wasted, wasted, wasted. I'm still saving sunflower seeds and packing up my BOMBSHELL BREASTS for a rainy day. I don't want my body to be wasted, wasted, wasted.

I looked at my watch and told Mike I had to go. "I'm so glad I met you. I think very highly of you—thank you for talking. I believe in what you're doing." When I said that, I meant it. We shook hands. If Doug could have seen this, he would have accused me of saying what I thought Mike wanted to hear. He would have said I was insincere. Little did he know that I'd never been more honest.

Life is a cheekpouch stuffed full of seeds.

The meaning of life is formed in that instant the tiny hamster foot takes the first baby step off the wheel. After that, it's all anticlimactic.

* * *

Loyalty is the color of a bruise.

From the time I was about 13 until I moved out once and for all, my mother took to her bed and refused to get out.

"I have a sinus headache. I can't do that now." Funny, she never had a "sinus headache" when my dad was in town. They only happened when he was gone.

She took to her bed, let the house deteriorate into a desertscape of dirty dishes, unwashed clothes, dusty furniture, mail-ordered Bible books, gardening equipment. The eye-watering benzene-ring TKO of Ben-Gay got locked up in the pore spaces of my favorite outfits. Those were the ones my mother invariably wore to the weekly devotional programs she organized and ran at the Rosewood Retirement Center—a euphemism for a smelly nursing home filled with the tragically senile, forgotten, or physically disabled elder citizens of this planet.

My mother looked better in my clothes than I did. I knew what Marlene Dietrich's zaftig daughter, Maria, must have endured with her glamour queen mother. My mother was a glamour queen once a week. The rest of the time, she was a messy-haired troll who menaced anyone who disturbed her in her bed.

But, hey. That was years ago. Don't I feel guilty remembering her flawed human nature? Yes. I do. I still feel the need to protect her, cover for her, lie for her, and be perfect for her. I can't abandon her. She will die without my clothes to wear to Rosewood. The memories are still so fresh— "Mother, can you take me to my piano lesson? It's raining." "No. Ride your bicycle. It's only sprinkling." "But, Mother!" "Shut the door. I have a sinus headache."

I never believed her. I always believed her.

I went outside, tied the dog's legs together with pantyhose and snickered as he tried to run away from me. Dear Buffy, my bucking bronco dog, my snow-white German Shepherd fool. While I had him tied up, I forced a little airline bottle of scotch down his throat.

"Mother, I'm going to my piano lesson now." On the way back, I stopped by the dime store and shoplifted beauty products. My favorite was the purple eye shadow. When I put it on the way I liked, it looked like I had been punched in the face. "Mother, I'm home." The silence was a slap in the face. "Mother—?"

The next day, I noticed the circles under her eyes were duller and more purplish-black than usual.

★ ★ ★

My hairshirt has fleas.

"You may not believe me. I know Doug doesn't believe me. But, God has put me here and I can't leave until He lets me go."

Doug's uncle was talking, but I wasn't listening. I was watching the heat radiate up from the parking lot of the Oasis Motel next door. A black man was unloading the trunk of his car. I pretended to be listening.

I decided that I, too, would try the monastic life. I believed myself ready for the Dark Night of the Soul. I could never be more ready for the cat-o'-nine-tails, walking on my knees, and fasting. It was easy before, why not now?

No one ever realized my sex games were my own personal Dark Night of the Soul. How could anyone realize it without my code book? My code book would explain my moves—how every conquest was really another lash to my back that would leave me bloody and in pain.

Percival suffered—he understood. His wisdom came at the end of his life, when he was confronting death. Mike is creating his own redemption in the form of a whip and a psychological lash. Maybe his code book would be worth reading after all. Our society, with its cultural symbols, whips us all, doesn't it?

I wanted Doug to love me, and I didn't want to go through all of this pain.

Mike's words echoed in my ears all the way back to Oklahoma.

Birth has put me here and will not let me go until He decides. Birth has put me on this earth and will not let me go until the body decides. Birth has put me here to suffer. The body will let me go when it decides. The body will liberate me.

What is liberation?

It was sounding suspiciously like Death. Don't you remember the scene in *Double Indemnity* when Edward G. Robinson tells Fred MacMurray that when two co-conspirators hook up together on a murder/insurance scam they're committed—it's a one-way trip that ends at the cemetery.

Boy, was he right.

Last week, a guy in Arizona took his three sons out into the mountains on a camping trip. Somewhere along the way, he decided they were possessed by the devil and he had to save them at all costs. This has a sadly predictable ending. He killed one. That was his way of chasing the devil out of his son. Then he decapitated the body.

The ribbon stretches ahead, falsely linear, like a map or a narrative. In Texas, I-35 is a road with borders, beginning at Oklahoma and the Red River, ending at the Gulf of Mexico. The coast of a shallow, quickly sedimenting body of water can be known for its storms, and it can be known for the squall lines one can call a force of nature or just more evidence of the devil at work in this phenomenal world.

I put on my hairshirt late at night, while thinking about Mike's code book, wondering again what my own codes are and why they torment me so much. The hairshirt scratches my breasts, and when it's hot, a thin stream of sweat forms in the curves. It dribbles down my ribs and I itch in a way that no amount of scratching can satisfy. If I drink a glass of wine, the hairshirt sheds tears and rubs the image of Percival into my heart. The pain is exquisite—it makes me think my life was worth living.

But one tiny flea adds too much and my nerves are flayed raw and ragged—I begin to beg for the end. I can't take it. Imagine. One flea can ruin everything. The flea is the devil. The devil is the flea. It's what it's like to be over the limit. You put fleas into your own hairshirt. Does that make you a devil, too?

Do you root out the "devil" by disowning it, saying it's in your son, then cutting off his head? I'm going too far. Stop me. I can't stop myself. I'm not able to meet my own needs. When? That's easy. When I hear that still, small voice calling me, saying "Your mother needs you. She will crumble and die without you. She will destroy you if you don't obey. You will starve, too." Birth put me here. Rebirth is not possible. My mother is through with labor.

Dependence imitates self-reliance. Independence imitates childishness.

Don't cut off my head. Just let me wear my own hairshirt. It's not a good one, since I don't know what the purpose of it is, or what I'm supposed to be able to do or control after I take it off. It's an unflattering shade of dog-fur brown. I doubt I'll learn much at this.

My hairshirt has fleas.

About the Author

Susan Smith Nash writes poetry, plays, and fiction. She currently teaches at the University of Oklahoma, where she received her Ph.D. in English Literature. The topic of her dissertation was doomsday literature.

A frequent traveller to Central and South America, she recently completed editing and translating an anthology of fiction, poetry, and essays by Paraguayan women writers.

Susan Smith Nash lives with her son in Norman, Oklahoma.

Other Trip Street Press Books

2000 and What?
A collection of 20 short stories about the turn of the millennium featuring both known and emerging writers of innovative fiction. What unifies these writers is their ability to avoid a predictable response to an inevitable event. Stories by Etel Adnan, Margaret Atwood, Frederick Barthelme, Lydia Davis, David Gilbert, Steve Katz, Kevin Killian, Donna Levreault, Harry Mathews, Ameena Meer, Susan Smith Nash, Niels Nielsen, Karl Roeseler, Teri Roney, Linda Rudolph, Kevin Sampsell, Lynne Tillman, Karen Tei Yamashita, Lewis Warsh, and Mac Wellman.

ISBN: 0963919229 $12.00

Five Happiness by David Gilbert
A 92-page puzzle of wit and audacious poetic technique by the author of *I Shot The Hairdresser*. A narrative extravaganza in which characters appear and disappear without warning. Fiction has never been so strange. "Captivating, brilliant prose that may be blinding to the normal eye." —*Kevin Sampsell*

ISBN: 0963919202 $6.95

The Adventures of Gesso Martin by Karl Roeseler
"Karl Roeseler takes a straightforward situation—a wandering rock star, a lion, seven French maids—and, with good humor and a charming light touch, rings magical changes on it. Particle by particle, with glittering clarity, the world of the fortunate Gesso Martin, the gentle chauffeur-cum-philosopher, gradually accumulates around us in an engagingly fantastic tale..." —*Lydia Davis*

ISBN: 0963919210 $8.95

Money Under The Table by Lewis Warsh
A collection of short stories from the author of *A Free Man* and *Private Agenda*. "Lewis Warsh's stories are devastatingly good. Fragments of plain unlikely lives are enacted in expertly simple, sinuous prose. Characters evolve in a bewitching and scary realm somewhere between event and insight, at the unnerving center of what we take to be reality. These people are all too convincing—we wouldn't want to be them, but we probably are." —*Harry Mathews*

ISBN: 09639192-3-7 $10.00

Order directly from our distributor Small Press Distribution (1-800-869-7553), from amazon.com, or from your favorite bookstore.

Trip Street Press is dedicated to the notion that a publisher's identity
only emerges through the juxtaposition of the books it publishes.